RICANTATIONS

ACKNOWLEDGEMENTS

Several of these poems, sometimes under other titles, have been previously published in journals and anthologies. Grateful acknowledgement is made to the editors:

Best American Poetry 2016; Bim; Caribbean Beat Magazine; The Caribbean Review of Books; The Caribbean Writer; A Congeries of Poetry, at Connotation Press; The Ekphrastic Review; Live Encounters; Moko: Caribbean Arts and Letters; PNR; The New Yorker; Past Simple; Poui: The Cave Hill Literary Annual; Puerto Rico en mi Corazón; Smartish Pace; Susumba's Book Bag; Under the Volcano/ Bajo el Volcán: The Best of Our First Fifteen Years; and *Vox Populi.*

My thanks to these book fairs, galleries, academic institutions, libraries, museums, poetry reading series, writing retreats and literary festivals: NYC: The New School; Trinidad & Tobago: Alice Yard; NGC Bocas Lit Fest; The North Coast Writing Retreat; Mt. Plaisir Estate Hotel; Medulla Art Gallery; St. Martin: St. Martin Book Fair; Barbados: Bim Lit Fest; Jamaica: Calabash Lit Fest; The Drawing Room Project; México: Under the Volcano; Jardín Borda de Cuernavaca, Morelos; Puerto Rico: Museo de Arte Contemporáneo; Aula Verde; El Archivo General; Poetry is Busy.

And special thanks to:
Ann-Margaret Lim, Luís Negrón, Millicent Graham, Jacqueline Bishop, Elidio la Torre Lagares, Nicholas Laughlin, Lasana Sekou, Shujah Reiph, Shivanee Ramlochan, Andre Bagoo, Richard Georges, David Knight, Jr., Willie Perdomo, Marcia Douglas, Alecia McKenzie, John Martínez, Geoffrey Philp, John R. Lee, Montague Kobbé, Robert Dupey, Maritza Stanchich, Leslie McGrath, Marty Williams, Pedro Pérez Osorio, Esther Philips, Tanya Savage, Magda Bogin, Dannabang Kuwabong, Sharon Leach, Lord Cloak, Michael La Rose, Faizah Tabasamu, and Marsha Pearce.

Give thanks to mentors and those who have encouraged or influenced the work: Philip Levine, Charles Hanzlicek, Larry Levis, William Matthews, Derek Walcott, Mark Wekander, Kwame Dawes, George Lamming, Paul Muldoon, Gerald Stern, Mervyn Morris, Kei Miller, Marvin Bell, and Jorie Graham.

My gratitude for Samuel Lind's permission to use his oil painting "Ángel Plenero" as cover art. Thanks also to artist Chemi Rosado Seijo for his inspiring community art project in Naranjito.

Thank you to Jeremy Poynting, Hannah Bannister, Kwame Dawes, and Adam Lowe of Peepal Tree Press.

Love to my children, Jeremy and Wenmimareba

LORETTA COLLINS KLOBAH

RICANTATIONS

PEEPAL TREE

First published in Great Britain in 2018
Peepal Tree Press Ltd
17 King's Avenue
Leeds LS6 1QS
UK

ISBN 13: 9781845234232

Supported using public funding by
ARTS COUNCIL
ENGLAND

CONTENTS

COME, SHADOW

yo sería boricano
aunque naciera en la luna

—Juan Antonio Corretjer
"Boricua en la luna"

NIGHT WATCH

Just at the moment
when the guard's
head droops sideways,
he hears the beating
windstorm of heavy,
feathered wings flogging
him to the ground,
then lifting off into the dark sky,
wings taller than a man,
smelling of seaweed and rot.

What was he guarding
but his own self, there in a ruined
grey hulk of the sugar central in Guánica,
out-of-use for forty years,
where even the tin signs cautioning
workers to use safety gear
and not lift more than they could bear
were hole-eaten with dusty mould?

The guard quits the next day,
in terror of being alone if it returns,
an iron-heeled gobbler landing on his shoulders,
wrapping him in its wing-bay, ascending.

If it is true, as witnesses claim,
that a red-eyed gargoyle broke free from the stone
rooftop of Nuestra Señora de Lourdes,
appearing later at that abandoned American mill,
and then stalked an old tobacco factory of Barranquitas,
where women and men once sat on the shed floor,
sewing together leaves for drying, baling,
and the rolling of three-cent cigars,
then it makes a kind of sense.

Why not show up here,
a gargoyle smelling of seaweed and sulphur,
a drop of moonlight in each ruby eye?
Perching on a roof of a company village –
where the sugarcane workers once dressed in the dark,
wrapping legs in burlap coffee bags, tying a piece of rope
around a hat – the gargoyle glimpses ghost girls playing
stick ball with a splintered fence post. He sees the way
a ghost son avoids the mandibles of the harvesting machine
as he carries a warm lunch in a fiambrera to his father
in the cane fields, or coffee and cheese,
or only coffee, if that was all to be had.

At the lechonera in Guavate, la gárgola
doesn't hawk-dive to steal
a roasted, salty pig from the spit.
He settles near the dance floor,
turning his long face to regard the man who
uses his hands to slaughter the pigs,
and then to the families holding hands,
twirling each other to merengue and salsa.
He chugs a pocket-bottle of Palo Viejo,
and then takes off like a crow.

In Carolina, he attacks a police officer
with no mercy – the official explanation
for why the cop discharged his gun,
showing up late after night-duty with a clawed face.

When the creature leaves our island,
flapping south to roost with Trinidad's jab-jabs,
our young men become gárgolas,
night creepers with diamond earrings,
perreando to reggaeton by Arcángel,
all gangster flow, dismantling girls in the disco.

Gatilleros of las Gárgolas, los pistoleros
of a mountain cartel from Gurabo, Guayama,
Caguas and Cayey, watch the keep of Castle Grayskull,
their own re-naming of the grey hulk
of a public housing residencial.
Their night-duty is asesinatos, guarding puntos de drogas.
They were still children just a few days ago,
playing stick ball, playing with toy guns
made out of sticks. Now they are gárgolas, flying
up our night streets, helmeted, red-eyed, on small motorbikes.

THE GREEN LANTERN Y LOS MUERTOS SENTA'OS

There's a club in Heaven
for all the puertorriqueños
who had a Ché Guevara t-shirt
in their closets when they died.

Sometimes Ché, himself, rides
on a float in their annual parade.
Every year, though, Carlos Cabrera
wins the title of *Coolest Ché-Impersonator.*

He gained his bantam-weight angel wings when
some cabrón clubbed his noggin with a baseball bat,
though his family called the event an accident.

At the wake, he sat up – sort of – meditating
with the incense of a half-smoked cigarette
that sagged from his fingers, his hands
on his knees, his legs hard-wired
into a Buddha pose, a Ché beret cap
with its lone silver star on his beat-up head,
his stitched eyes concealed by black sunglasses.

It is true that his head drooped,
out-of-alignment from the bat strikes.
He did look cool, though, during his night vigil
in the basketball court of Caserío San José,
but after that, his wired legs never straightened out.
Even as an angel, he has to take little hops,
like a levitating yogi, to circumambulate Kingdom Come.

Some undertaker at Funeraria Marín,
an artist, fashion designer or store window
mannequin-dresser at heart,
a transformista of youths peppered with ammo,

bends bodies into action figures for coffin-less velorios.
                    And so, Christopher,
who in life lost more boxing matches
than he won, a veritable knockout punchbag,
was propped up, stiff in golden satin shorts,
in a boxing ring, his eyes, behind sunglasses,
eyeballing invisible Death in the opposite corner,
who was already victorious, getting a rub down
from a couple of his hottie angels of Death.

                              In Heaven, though,
este chulo is unstoppable. First, he wrestles Jacob,
punching his hip socket on the inner sinew of the thigh.
Then, he choke-holds the angel who wrestled Jacob.
Angels and cherubim crawl away, overcome
with concussions and dislocated wings,
until the Heavenly Promoters decree,
by unanimous decision, that Christopher
must hang up his gloves, appointing him
Harbinger of the Technical Knockout,
and tossing him, in disgrace, through the clouds,
back to Puerto Rico, to the boxing program
of the Departamento de Corrección
y Rehabilitación, where various convicts
enjoy repeatedly beating his unparadisaical ass.

The truth is, God, or the First Science Officer
of God, was looking for a soul to send
to be a true Guardian Angel of Puerto Rico,
seeing as how both Spain and the U.S.
had so fucked the job up. It was a kind
of treaty, or promesa, between the Promised Land
and D.C. Comic's Guardians of the Universe.

The next candidate was el Señor Velásquez Velásquez.
He and his pal were volunteering

13

for the Civil Defense of Trujillo Alto.
He played a practical joke on his compañero,
which caused the other volunteer guard some pain
in the groin. This made that guy shoot
his regulation Glock pistol model 19 caliber
9 millimeters into Señor Velásquez Velásquez.
                                        Funeraria Marín
posed him in one of the ambulances of his company,
cigarette in hand, in black glasses, windows sealed.
Angel Recruitment Office thought it a sad case,
but in the end, el Señor Velásquez Velásquez
failed the driving test for Guardian Angels because
boricuas in Heaven drive their glorymobiles
just like they drive down here, not one of them
ever pulling over for an ambulance siren.
Señor Velásquez Velásquez is still stuck
in a south-central heavenside traffic jam.

Georgina Chervony, dead in her rocking chair,
dressed in her bridal gown, made such a grandmotherly
angelita that all the children and viejitos verdes
of Heaven asked her to stay.

That left Renato García, whose last breath
abandoned him lying on the pavement
behind a restaurant. All of his neighbours
from the community of San José,
in *Renato Green* t-shirts at the home wake,
gave him a big send-off with plena music, singing
Raphy Leavitt's "La Cuna Blanca," *Ay, Angelito escapado.*

He stood in his sister's home,
in his Green Lantern suit and mask,
one hand in fist-salute over his heart.
Everyone knew Renato was not thinking

of the wrongs that had been done to him in life,
or any other superhero stuff.

Bueno, Bueno, Bueno, nada de malo,
Friends and neighbours all knew Renato,
who, after he found the suit of Linterna Verde
in a trash can of cast-off clothes, had worn it daily
on the streets of Barrio San José, and could always be
called on for a favour, to help with this or that,
to carry loads, fetch a litre of milk,
to sweep a store step. He was servicial.

Perfectability may not be attainable,
but his attempt was measured in his sister's
utterance. Praise enough. That is how his matter,
upon his death, became pure energy, a green light
that could meld into any form.

When he arrived at the gates of Heaven,
green-lit clouds preceded him.
St. Peter was not there with the keys
to the Kingdom, but the greeter wore
the Ring of the Lion of Judah, *Irie! Selah!*
The angel looked at the Green Lantern ring
on Renato's finger and his aura of green light.

This is how Renato was chosen to be sent
back to Puerto Rico. If you see S.W.A.T. riot police
involuntarily dancing the Macarena,
lassoed in light, while the pueblo marches,
and the helicopters sky-write messages
of hope, it is Renato's handiwork.
In the times of austerity that are coming,
may we all be serviciales – known in our communities
for our everyday, glimmering works.

TISSUE GALLERY

On the fifth floor
of the medical school,
sequestered from public view,
a black slab lab table
lined with old apothecary and twist-top jars
sealed with paraffin wax,
a shoal of *not-fish* treading bronzy water,
each homunculus labelled
in terms of in-utero days and weeks.

In this jarscape, a palm-size one
sitting with legs crossed,
arms raised protectively,
clasping the top of his head
like a child expecting blows in a parental brawl,
and this golem, a perfect mini-person,
holds fingers curved lightly in front of him,
as if playing a piano chord,
and this *quelque chose* has blackened soles –
in the womb,
a douen meant to range the barefoot forest,
those faceless stillborn and early-dead children
with backward feet,
who lure human playmates to the woods
and fill their always hungry mouths with little crabs.

All casualties are clipped
with yellowed plastic navel clamps
that look like bones.
Here are twins, one larger than the other,
one malformed
with a hydrocephalitic-fissured face,
and this one's wrinkly forehead,
the face of a worried eighty-year-old concentrating

on his death, an extra epaulette flap on his shoulder,
                              as if he is sprouting wings;
triplets like three piglets,
                         one with lots of hair,
one with a cauliflower, puckered ear, one
with a purple-black hand reaching out of the water,
              as if in hope of rescue from drowning.

The thirty-six-weekers are not stored in glassware.
A perfect pair, girl and boy, are on separate cookie baking sheets,
          wrapped in sterile pads, their swaddling blankets.
They are not desiccated, withered, mummified,
              quick-frozen, frost-nipped, or sealed in wax.
They look like leatherette dolls in mid-kick,
          stop-motion animation,
                    as if they'd only now stopped breathing.

Girl was a low birth-weight,
vagina snapped as tightly shut as the seam of a walnut.
Boy is not the colour of life, a rich-coloured brown boy
              bleached out to plasticine-pale, dun-white.
Still, on his cheek-ear-hair, the almost-feel of life.
     The abdomen is caved-in,
and the testicles are paper-thin, black crumpled leaves.

Some in the jars were named and tagged on the wrist.
     I was told that I cannot tell you the names.
          It is a secret between the women
                    and these medical anomalies.
          One is named for a hurricane.

The restos muertos have closed eyes and African features.
     They were not colourfast,
     so the chemicals have bleached them to albino.
The women, who came with gravid uterus
          to Puerto Rico from the Virgin Islands,
seeking to save or end pregnancies,

17

do not know that these small ones are still here
          curled in their womb-poses,
     each blanched in its lit-glass aquarium,
lolling in solutions the colour of beer, brandy,
          honey, oil or perfume.

These small floating gods in primer paint,
          never to be besprinkled
               with blessed water to help them crossover,
never to evaporate, dust-scatter, or waste —
          they are here and not here!
               What is the shelf-life of the unborn?

In the Caribbean, women must travel
          from island to island to get needed health care,
          and so these doodads
               were not carried home, but donated,
               no one knows how long ago.

I have been invited here by a doctor who loves
          the arts, and whom I like.
I was told beforehand only that I would be viewing
          human tissue.
He proposes collaboration,
     an artistic public exhibition
          of these impossible children,
               who will never utter "peacock", "butterfly",
                    "confetti", "crazy quilt", "cashmere", or "soap".
                         Skullduggery.
Monster Midway. Gaff joints. Shell games.
          Sideshow piebald children.
               Human oddities and the science of teratology.

          At home, I whisper to the midnight page,
Women of the Virgin Islands, Sistren,
               I saw them, and they are okay.
     Your small ones are still on the Earth!

LA MONSTRUA DESNUDA

Oiled glow of swagbelly, the dimpled
pillars of her legs, calf flesh cuffing
ankles, young puffed pouches of breasts —

for three hundred and forty-six years,
Eugenia's body has been admired
as a prodigy of nature, in arcades
of buffoons, dwarves and men of pleasure.

An empire's loaner, she crossed seas
to hang temporarily in this island space.
Curvature of the inflated globe of her middle —
brushed with crushed pearls, so that,
back-shadowed in black, she's lit from within.

It was mercy on himself, the painter, or for the child
posed nude against the table, to put in her hand
a stem of black grapes from Asturias,
to wrap her vulva in three leaves,
and crown her with grapevines.

Una niña gigante —
abnormality styled as a baroque Bacchus.

In a room of paintings by Velázquez,
I stand by Eugenia for a long time.
I morph into a sculpture of Eugenia,
for never in this Earth's constant flash
of images have I seen so purely
and perfectly a likeness of myself —

Eugenia Martínez Vallejo,
born in Bárcenas, given up by her parents
at El Alcázar in Madrid to marvel
the royal court and dwell in its protection.

She was six years old, abandoned plaything
of el Rey Carlos II, himself un inválido,
barely able to rule, but under whom
herds of humans were carried to quemaderos,
burning places of the auto-de-fé.

The court ordered Juan Carreño de Miranda
to paint two portraits of la monstrua,
una desnuda y una vestida de gala.

Eugenia stood undressed for the painter,
but she didn't yield, enfant terrible
with hyperphagia. She averted red face
in a cut-eye of pout and rage.

Carreño de Miranda painted white dashes
on her lower eyelids that will never
spill over into tears.
I live in the sneer of her face.

Gawked at girl, phenomenal weight
advertised in the press, a child displayed
for royal visitors, naked Eugenia.
Orphaned, how long did you live at court?
How long did you live?

La monstrua vestida painted
in a red brocade dome of a dress,
red rotunda, red bloated brass bell –
expanding red giant –
you could pick her up by the head
and ring out the hour.

In each grabby, hoggish hand,
she holds a red apple, quenchless
hunger of the Spanish Empire

embodied in one girl.
One apple for Spain
and one for Puerto Rico.
Eugenia was the ripest apple on the tree.

Carlos II had no children.
Were there children at the court
to pinch her and pull her around
by her red hair-ribbons?
Weakened by Prader-Willi,
if she fell asleep under a window,
did someone lug her to bed?

Eugenia and the dwarves will return
to el Museo de Prado, but I will keep
a postcard of Eugenia in my bag.
I notice other women like me,
and now I note people with achondroplasia,
wherever I go: one hoisting a computer
overhead in a hallway of the medical school;
two dwarves driving mini street-sweepers,
one with corn-rowed hair in a meridian
on prison detail, one riding a bike,
carrying across the handlebars
a lead pipe for those who gape;
Calle 13's bailarina Karlita
holding a tall ice cream cone.

We are the big and small people
of the world, Obatalá's children,
still anomalies, the freaky-freaky of sideshows.
We don't fit what is built
and bargained for in this world.

Eugenia is my fierce beauty and force,
so I'll claim la estética de lo feo –

my own baroque body misshapen, obese,
sometimes an iron maiden of pain,
something I drag, heave, roll and sway.

Oiled gleam of swagbelly, the dimpled
pillars of my legs, calf flesh cuffing
ankles, puffed pouches of breasts –
the everyday looks, the uninvited words often said.
Soy una esteticista comprometida de lo feo.
Eugenia's postcard rides in my purse,
like a pocket manifesto, a red grenade.

COME, SHADOW

After two years on the other side,
she gave up on visiting my dreams –
then a decade of non-intervention,
quiet ashes in a buried tin box.

Today, she is detectable
in my peripheral vision,
everywhere in my head
– annunciation.

Singing *Yellow bird*
up high in banana tree
with me on her lap
in a padded rocker
in front of the wide window,
where we waited up late
for my father to come home.

She is taking me,
at this hour, to the plastic bit
in her mouth that she must bite.
We had an electric metal coffee pot
with a short in the frayed cord. I was small.
I touched the spout with a wet finger,
and the current jumped into me and shook me.
I couldn't move my hand or my feet.
Is that what the shock was like?
                              A body
thrown against an electrified fence,
convulsions hard enough to break bones
against each other or pop them out of sockets?
Did she receive anaesthetic, muscle relaxers,
soothing syrups or a salve for her temples?

I remember the room full of women.
When mother arrived, she wore a half-slip
and bra. Her hair was cut short, lopped off.
Conversation undiscoverable. Vague hands
of the women who wanted to touch me
and pull me, rag baby, to them.
All had short hair and were not fully dressed.
I was afraid of them and for them.
I was in a tight space, like
a bathroom full of steam. I had to get out.

I remember the long lawn of the state hospital
and the willow tree that I sat under.
Mother had drawn a paper doll
for me with fold-over tabs on its dresses.
It looked like a woman who had jumped
out of her skin – green and black veins
crayoned on its arms and legs. I held onto it.
It is what I had of my mother on the car ride home.

Today, she is not quelled, chastened or hushed.
I see her in the women's ward
of the state psychiatric hospital,
where she stayed that time for a year,
ambushed, labelled a paranoid schizophrenic,
tackled, injured and carried off by police
in my kindergarten year.

Stanchions hold against her fury,
evasive, sly fox lover of the Holy Ghost,
who is here with her, like a plasma flame.
That Holy Ghost is visible, manifest,
speaking to her, keeping her alive,
dashing Molotov cocktails of sexual hunger
against her body.
                    She is cinched to the bed.
She is corseted into restraint jackets.

She is Mommy-tucked tightly in wet blankets.
She is naked in the showers with the other women.
She is high-dosed with antipsychotics and suppressors
of side effects, in the name of our Father,
O, Holy Haldol, Lithium, Meleril and Valium.
She sleeps, she drools, my jaw shakes,
my hands tremble. I scream words.
There are many beds in my room.

In a room of bathtubs, she is trussed into a canvas hammock,
suspended for an hour in a bath filled with hot water –
forced to be recumbent by small nurses,
ham-handed nurses, orderlies, and psych techs.
Hot water to smooth the cloven hoof,
body that must relent in the warm cradle,
blunted, limp, trodden under, steamrolled.
If not, fill the bath with ice and icy water,
woman numbed to unriddling in the sling stretcher.
I see two rows of bathtubs in the long room,
a woman's cropped head sticking out
above the canvas tarp covering each one.

I see the sessions with the doctor,
who thumbs through her thoughts,
skims over her terrors, probes a teenage rape
in the forest, her love of God, her husband's errors,
and, then, prescribes the 18th round
of electroconvulsive shock therapy before
he walks to the staff cafeteria for lunch.

This day is in 1966, and the present year, the 50th
since my mother was strapped to the laboratory table,
electrodes placed at her temples and chest, a gag –
a plastic bit in her mouth to prevent tongue swallowing
and teeth breakage.
                    I see the dials on the machine
that someone will have to set for intensity,

the levers that someone will have to turn on
for a duration until she reaches the crescendo,
her whole body a stiff divining rod,
that then jerks in mal seizures, until, in fact,
she leaves her body and billows above it,
a blue-grey shadow of a sail, like the Holy Ghost.

I hear skeletal tones of every bone jack-hammered
like a brass gong.
                    Whether she is conscious
or unconscious, she feels as if she can't breathe.
She cannot breathe, and she is dying.
But she does not die. She is bruised, softened –
not cured, but vulcanised.

On the day of the visit that I remember,
she tells my father he must talk to Dr. Patel
because if she has another
shock treatment, she will die.
It will be months before she is home, though,
and she will be hospitalised uncountable times
after that.
                    She will remember the far past,
but misremember and blank out on yesterday,
last week, the days of my girlhood pixelated,
in her electrocuted memory of gaps.
What are we but moment and memory?

Quite out of nowhere,
my mother has chosen to come back, today –
to pick out my memories
like meat slivers in boiled crab.
My own children are grown.
Perhaps mother means to stay with me
this time, for my home stretch.

Shadow, go back.
I'm not your horse.

WINGED HORSE

A gruff nickering and lip-flap
comes from the horse standing
at my back gate again, biting the railing
of chainlink that hems in
the tamarind on my patio from him.
I like that horse sound when I'm in bed.

During the day, he is tied to a white tree trunk
with no sun canopy in the open field behind my gate.
Though it's not ours, the land is a commons
for my neighbours, a pasture skirted by tulip trees.
In the field, Armando, my neighbour, shoots an air rifle
and lets his pit bull Pepé run after rats.

Although he pulls no millstone, the stallion walks
slow circles around the tree, a swath where grasses
have been eaten down to baked clay.
His water bucket lies on its side.
In my mind, I have bought a tarp
and tied it from the treetop to my fence
to shade him. In my mind, I have filled
a trough with barley, corn, oats, and beet pulp,
pulled green-topped carrots from my pockets
to feed him through the patio fence,
this down-at-heel, derelict horse
with many grey ticks embedded
in his forehead, neck and breast,
rows of fat ticks corn cobbing his skin.

Though his eyes are deep and his face
and soft nose as attractive as that of any horse,
he is a bare scaffold of a horse. His back
vertebrae and eighteen ribs are visible –
the shoulder scapular and hip bones

poke up, where the skin covering them is thin
and hair-scraped and shabby –
tatty chestnut pelt of a taxidermised horse.
The hip bones are so shrink-wrapped
by his hide that I look up horse anatomy
to name these bones the wings of Ilium.

Sometimes he drags the rope behind him,
let loose to forage weeds beyond his circle.
Broken down in the pasterns, fetlock-hurt, joints
disjointed, he hobbles on front hooves
that don't stand squarely on the ground
but angle up.
              Sometimes, the owner drives
our street in his yellow pick-up truck,
rattling its rack, horse ropes and butt chains.
He fights with my neighbour about the boarding
of the horse. Men yell, "Es mi derecho."

Sometimes at twilight, when I come home,
the horse is tethered to a teeter-totter
in the children's playground across the street.
He stays there all night, nibbling short grass.
When he walks, unminded, in the street,
I call to him from my high window; he whinnies.
In my mind, I have seen him put down.
But, he is so full of life!
In my mind, I have faced the anger
of the bellowing men and rescued him.

I rescued a sato once, a feral dog,
fierce, with her five pups.
I visited a sanctuary, hundreds of shrieking
and barking and yowling dogs penned
in full Caribbean sun, with just two fans.
I am in dog-hell, I said to myself.

The sound of the dogs was misery.
I couldn't wait to get out of there.

Last night, the moon sat in the sky
like a bowl. I had to look up moon phases
to name it an upward-opening crescent moon.
It was like a glass calabash of glowing milk.
I thought of the Buddhist begging bowl.
It was Sunday night when neighbours put
their trash out for Monday collectors.

At midnight, the horse was dipping his head
into each blue barrel that neighbours
had set out. He gobbled white plastic bags.
He pulled our rotten bones out of each can.
When I saw him, he had already fed
from all the trash bins along our street.
I watched from my upstairs window
how he used his teeth to lift out each item.
He filled storm drains and gutters with our detritus.
I walked down my stairs and into the street.
I called to him, but he walked down the hill
in that uneven gait he has. I didn't hear his horsey
blabbering all night. Today he is not tied to the tree.
In my mind, I see how he opened Styrofoam boxes
and licked food traces. There are many
horses living in this city. People do not leave
them behind in the countryside.
I name this horse Rocinante,
those arguing men, rocín. He is not mine
to name. Rocinante!
I am broken-down, too.
A woman and a hard keeper horse
sharing this space on Earth, for a time.

ONE THAT GOT AWAY

Miguel's boat is tied to a mangrove pier
under ilán-ilán trees by the bay.
He used to carry me through the city
on inland waterways, trawling canals
that pass under low bridges, through mangroves,
where fishermen hurl hoop-nets from the bank,
and crabs roost on overhanging branches,
through the estuaries and lagunas,
to islets where white egrets nest,
the water-road of Suárez, sometimes clogged
with jetsam, flood-gathered twigs, cast-off cans,
rubbish strewn from San Juan to Piñones.
Miguel, a pescador-artesano,
ran his fishing boat in San José bay,
near the coast of Bahía de San Juan,
or by el Frente Marítimo de Cataño,
away from ferry and cargo ship lanes.
A carved wooden mermaid hung on the wall
of his dockside locker, hand-painted, pink,
with blue wimple cloth wrapped around her head,
breasts round like shooter marbles with red dots
for the nipples and peach aureolas,
and a mossy fan-tail scaled in green-gold.
Fashioned from a block of that sweet-smelling
female cedar tree, cut by Miguel under a waning moon,
she was to bring him good luck, safe sailing.
When he didn't fish, he turned a wood lathe
to make pilones, wooden mortar cups
for crushing herbs or mashing mofóngo.
He carved celestial santos, la mano
poderosa, a rough, pierced hand of Christ,
divine family chiselled on fingertips.
He whittled sirens to bless the prows
of the motor boats of his compañeros.

I rode in a folding chair placed down centre
in his boat, around which he worked with Jaime.
In the mornings, before the sun stunned us,
Miguel worked without his shirt, sweat-slicked back
with la Vírgen del Carmen, the Mother
of Fishermen, full-colour, stitched into his skin,
a token for mercy, a mantle, Stella Maris
glazed radiantly on his labouring back.
Once he caught a shark, gaffing it, hauling
it into the boat at my feet, cutting from head to tail.
Much blood muck. Iron smell of blood.
On nights of fiestas patronales
in Cataño, I helped Miguel sell saints,
mer-women, and drinks at a kiosk.
Many fishing boats crowded the dark bay,
a bobbing armada lit by one skiff
strung with coloured lights, carrying a priest
and, at the stern, a Vírgen del Carmen
adorned with ribbons, bundles of flowers.
Miguel's tumorous leg, amputated at the knee –
botched, foundering, a slow suppuration.
His sister had sewn from flowered fabric
a loose thigh sock and trimmed it with red lace
for the blanched stump of the irradiated leg.
He removed it, showing me the surgeon's cut,
the meat peeled back to rod the femur shaft,
a titanium rod forced and tapped into
the cavity of bone. Atrophied stub.
The strong pain medication worked at first.
But, then it didn't.
When radiation therapy began,
he kept on fishing. And then, he didn't.
The treatments burned calf flesh beyond healing.
Skin and muscle didn't come back to life.
María del Carmen, in extremis,
Nuestra Señora, Estrella de los mares,

Salvage me from spoilage, gangrene, guárdame.
But, she didn't.
See his neuralgic hands, pins and needles
in fingers folded around a Medalla,
unable to sculpt sweet smelling cedar.
Cancer kept spreading its net. It carved him.
Miguel spoke of the new prosthetic leg
that he would be fitted with in a week.
But, he wouldn't be.

At papal inaugurations, I've read,
a fisherman's ring is bestowed upon
the new pope to signify his mandate.
I imagine it wrought of yellow-rose gold,
thick, reed-hammered, inset with sapphires
or a marquise diamond, a fisherman
engraved there in aquamarine pavé.
Miguel loved it when his boat passed under
branches and blooms of ilán-ilán trees,
where not even fish reek could overcome
the sudden sweet, jasmine-custard fragrance.
Whenever I smell ilán-ilán scent-drift
while driving past a tree-lined boulevard
or walking my girl across her school yard,
or like now, queasily watching water
lap below the pier through gaps in wooden slats,
I think of the small boat catching sunlight
in the mangrove canals, and him, singing,
a young fisherman at work with his seine –
a bright and colourful virgin standing
on her sickle moon and heads of cherubs
on his muscled back. Miguel, you are this hush.
You are my walk on the shore of the bay.
Fish blood.

JUSTINE HAS A FEW WORDS
FOR THE MARQUIS DE SADE

For one year
after the lightning
I dreamed about women
sleeping between bread knives.

The point is

The point is

beyond the rocks. I have stopped dreaming
and whatever you want

just want.

I have waded out today

past the silt edge

where it gets deeper.

Have peeled my suit
down past my hips.

The sunbathers baked on the rocks
can see nothing through this dark water.

You can see nothing,
not the faint scars

under one breast.

I had a simple life,
like an old ballad:

I walked out crying
past city skylines.

I sat in a hay loft
like a maid.

I knew how to balance milk pails.

I wandered the cliffs
looking for oyster scows,
submarines and whalers.

I remember drunks, hibiscus minced
like my grandmother's torn petticoats,

like drummers after a battle,
like the red satin shoe
I found in the gulley.

My shoulders are cold
under water.
The sun is warm in California.
The sun is warm in San Juan.

Even if you follow me here

Even if you follow me here

     I remember mother
     dressing at the sink.
     Chet Atkins on the radio,
     Eddie Palmieri on the radio,
     Javier Rosas on the radio,
     with accordions and sousaphones.

On any street
you might bump against

me, a woman straightening
her skirt, suddenly
a face you remember.

I'm the arm
moving carefully
through the roses,
trinity spines of bougainvillea,

the garter hitched
up behind
the café counter.

Not
the woman parked at a gasolinera
in Death Valley

dialling your number.

Not
the woman splayed in the vineyard.
Not the woman split in the cane.

(Never
La Mujer de los Trovadores
devoured by hounds).

I like to read and sleep
after a swim.

That's my face
reading in yellow light
by the window
on the third floor
above the train depot.

The sky smells like geraniums.
The air smells like my blood days.
My breath smells like a bakery.
The air grows thinner.

Your train is pulling out.

I don't own anything
but a few ribbons

and my own scars.

You can't touch them.

Your train is pulling out,
pendejo,
and you're on it, I said.
I wrote the book
in my lap.

I won't look up.
Dale poder a un pendejo
y será tu verdugo.

NIGHT OF CHARCOAL SKY AND SEA

One dim pole-lamp
                lit the malecón.
— raining.
           Dollar bills
                folded
                        were water-glued to the pavement.
                I looked,
        but I didn't pick them up.
I kept walking   alone
                        along the malecón.
A man followed me,
                        close at my elbow.
He wore a knit cap,
                a green army jacket.
He was close to my book bag.
My wallet
        was on the ground, but
                                I couldn't find it.
He spoke in a quiet voice.
                        He wanted money.
He smiled once.
I told him
        about the wet dollars,
                on the malecón.
He looked back,
                but leaned on my elbow.
I was walking, and then
                        he wasn't there. I heard
the sea; it sounded like
                it would crest onto the malecón.
I walked to El Makito.
                No fishermen were docked,
        drinking or dozing in their boats.
I stood at the rail of the malecón.

A friend
         whom I used to desire
    was holding a miniature rabbit.
She was my rabbit,
              so I took her from him.
She climbed
         onto my shoulders
    and half-slipped out of my hands. Then,
there were dogs.
First, a small mutt
         growling and trying to lunge.
Sunlight was intense.
              A German shepherd ran
         across the grass.
I blocked him with my hip.
              I wanted to punch his head.
His mouth was trying to bite,
         his long nose coming at me.
He harried me,
              jumping against me.
    The rabbit was slipping from my grip.
I called the woman to get her dogs.
         She stood in a yellow dress and red apron
in the bright doorway of her house.
She didn't call the dogs.
                   She just looked at me
from across her front lawn.
              And then, she called
    the monster, *Dante, Dante, Dante.*

I was at the pier at twilight.
    A woman at the boat ramp
         walked into the dark water.
              She put her small son
         into a kayak the size of a yellow cradle.
The water was lit
         only with one long line of golden light.

Each small wave in the beam-path
            was shining.
Wooden logs and telephone poles, charred
            and saturated with creosote,
        floated in the congested water.
                They bumped against each other,
                those tossing poles.
She walked amidst them.
                    There was a long fish —
gun-grey — shaped
        like a heavy barracuda or a pike,
            holding still against the current,
    a few feet away from the woman.
She was singing a lullaby.
            It rose up over the waves.
            I could hear it.
                    It was soothing, but
        not something
I had heard before.
        I think she was improvising.
        She was breast-high
                in the water, and walking.
    The wooden beams rolled
            over her. She shifted
        the kayak over each black log,
still wading to the sea.
I saw a fish as long as a telephone pole.
                I don't think it was alive.
        It, too, was charred
            and tar-smudged in thick creosote.
It floated side-by-side with the poles.
            The boy saw the fish
            and shouted out to his mother.
She kept humming and moving out into the sea.

BLUE STONE

I.

A bullet zinged
over homes of Villa Palmeras
to enter the brain of Karla Michelle
          on New Year's Eve —

over clothes festooning terraces,
families eating while abuelita's album
of El Grand Combo played
on the old stereo of the marquesina.

I find a blue woman painted two lanes over
from where Karla fell,
                    Legba's X on a concrete wall.
The graffitero,
          poet laureate of gunshot,
                    draftsman of spirit,
incised his stone vision
          and opened the portals.
                    He prepared the way,
                              marked the spot.

Her face is monument, blue African mask —
mouth, nose and ear — flesh, more than stone.

In the mural, she is dying, a fallen idol,
a tumbled statue. Just one colossal stone head
tilted sideways on the ground,
with a fractured face flooded by moonlight.

The mural, painted two years before the bullet
entered Karla's brain,
          called the bad shot

to this zone just as surely as vèvès
            painted in ash and cornmeal call gods.

In the mural, Blue Stone
            has bullet-entrance holes
        drilling into her forehead and cheek.

Blue Stone is wreathed with laurel,
            or funerary garland or seaweed.
Is she Yemayá washed in from the sea?

I want the blue goddess to rise up
            from that wall.
Let her eyes open wide
        and light up –
finding the celebratory hand that held the gun.
        I don't want vengeance
or to hear his confession.

I want the man who celebrated New Year's Eve
by firing a shot high into the air to see the parents
of Karla Michelle, holding each other close,
in the nave of their mutual suffering.

I want the man whose bullet entered the brain
of Karla Michelle to put a gardenia flower
in a wooden toy boat and set it out to sea,
praying for renewal,
every New Year's Eve,
for as long as he lives.
I will receive it.

II.

Declared brain-dead,
Karla Michelle was costumed
    like the Virgin Mary
        in sky-blue veil.
At the public wake,
  in the Park of the Salsa Kings,
    where busts of singers
  look like tombstones –
      Rafael Cortijo and Tommy Olivencia
    Pellín Rodríguez, Ismael Rivera
      and Hector Lavoe –
    Tito Puente shining like a new penny –
      the town stood under tents,
  out of the rain falling like bullets.

On festooned horse cart, her casket rolled by mourners.

Police used a 360° camera to photograph the neighbourhood.

It only revealed sagging awnings,
        a boy and his uncle working
    under their car.

If the camera had pulled back,
to a larger ring of the bull's-eye target,
      it would have recorded
  the Blue Stone mural,
one more pushpin on our Map of Carnage.

REVEL REBEL

HE TALKS TO A BUTTERFLY

Joe harvests eggs in the copulario,
where monarchs and orange fritillaries
achieve butterfly positions
without the *Karma Sutra,* profusely
boogalooing in air. Male claspers
grapple la mariposa's *ductus bursae,*
on milkweed tufts and passion vines,
to the sad boleros and waltzes
of Paquitín Soto and his trio singers,
which Joe plays over loudspeakers.
He watches butterfly lovers
bumble romance, clumsily
facing away from each other.

Joe tends caterpillars wagging tentacles
as they shimmy along his fingers, and when
new butterflies arrive head-down into the world,
like we do, he flings open barn windows
of the grey loft to liberate them
into the netted ginger-lily gardens of the mariposario.

He is the caretaker of this low-security pen,
where more sailing refugees escape
than stay hemmed in. A free colony
of hundreds roosts in windbreak trees
at the edge of the pasture. A platoon
of butterflies searches
the mesh tent for a way back
into paradise.

Released from prison into the butterfly farm,
Joe came here as an ex-con.
A monarch egg has a 10% chance,
maybe 3%, of producing an adult
who survives. Eighty prisoners

were released into the farm
to mind the garden, to look with wonder
at life having its own way,
at wings floating
in the Koi fish pond.

Joe is the one who stayed,
even after funds for the programme
dried up in the next election.

Monarch caterpillars
eat a milkweed leaf each day
and the garden can't produce enough.

So every weekend, Joe drives
along the island's north coast, looking
for more milkweed plants.

Two purple scars
indent his cheek — as if flaming fingers
once held his face, trying to crush it —
slug holes somewhat healed.

When he explains why he still shows up
at the farm to do what he can
for orphaned winged things,
he just says, *Me fascinan.*

> One day, someone will arrive
> to take the keys away from him
> and shut the place down.

For now, a butterfly grips his fingertip.
It flutters, lifting high over red lilies,
humming, sotto voce, a bolero, *I am going
far from here, voy con el alma hecha pedazos
you won't forget me, and I won't forget you…*

FLOWERS AND SONGS

for Elena

I slept in the hot afternoon, draped in a green serape;
a book of poems by women imprisoned
in Atlacholoaya, Morelos – campesinas mexicanas
y mujeres indígenas – fluttered open on my breasts
like the spread wings of a bird dust-bathing in the shade
of this bougainvillea trellis. Craving hibiscus juice,
I slept after reading a song about infusions of herbs
that heal us, leaf of the guayaba, el epazote,
el manrubio, and our own hierba buena.

It is not hurricane season on my island;
sea breezes come and go quietly.
Yet such a wind woke me, singing loudly
through the flowers and rattle-seed pods
of the blue jacaranda hanging over my chair,
that same wild wind that came in the nights,
crying down through deep crevasses of the mountains,
the minaret rocks of Tepoztlán, in the morning-dark,
when sounds of the pueblo, church bells,
bass-booms of fireworks, weddings, brass bands,
cantinas, dogs, goats, motorbikes, roosters,
and turkeys had all simmered down.
There, I brewed chocolate to warm me
against that wind and wrote at a table
where I kept clay jars of roses.

Wakened, I think of my sisters of Morelos,
incarcerated women of Atlacholoaya
who have found words to sing to their lost children,
to mothers, to the bristled moustaches of their men.

Twenty years of teetering on scaffolding
it took for Diego Rivera to add the last brush dab

47

to the nostrils of terra cotta indios, ivory Spaniards
in his Cuernavaca mural adorning the fortress walls
of Cortés, where Emiliano Zapata Salazar,
son of Morelos, poses on one pillar,
brandishing bandoliers and sabre.

I, too, love Zapata, his revolt against the poverty
and serfdom of indios and campesinos;
his fight for liberty and land, to divide up
the property of the sugar hacendados.
Who does not like to hear Lucha Moreno
or Amparo Ochoa sing the corridos
of la soldadera Adelita, la Marieta o la Rielera?
Those women who rode horseback with Zapata,
riders of hurtling horses; in long dresses or breeches,
soldaderas Zapatistas crossed-their-hearts
with brassieres of bullets,
padded their hips with pistols,
shouldered rifles, pulled the trigger.

Flowers and songs and corridos,
but this poem is not for Adelita,
or Zapata.

It is for my friend, Elenita,
who champions the prisoneras,
who holds writing classes at Atlacholoaya;
who publishes penitentiary art, poems and memoirs.

In forced reclusion, perhaps a woman wants
just the smell of coffee, gardenias,
and the *"azalea-honey"* of a lover's skin;
the cleaned, pressed cotton smell
of a night-shirt; a healing tea of el epazote,
or hierba buena; her children's faces; dignity,
redemption, to be useful, to be loved; to be free.
She wants a quiet space

where she can gather her words and send them flying
through cell bars like yellow petals blown
on hard wind, on red macaw wings.

Elena de Hoyo Pérez of Cuernavaca,
in the State of Morelos, you are beautiful.
You are not following Zapata.
The prisoneras follow you.
Their poems are hoof-beats, a hard, cantering wind.
Why have I given so few thoughts to the women
in the penal colonies of Puerto Rico?
A colony within a colony.
As you say, Elena,
They are women
just like me, just like you.
Any one of us could be inside there.
Any woman could do
what they have done.

SONG OF THE HARPY

Maybe it's true that we were eating paella,
singing along with the bohemia music,
sipping a bucket of iced cervezas under pink sky
at La Playa los Machos, our toes sifting
shell fragments out of the sand,
when the truck backed up to our table.
Emergency Management of Ceiba, DRNA,
and in the back, a rhesus macaque in a wire cage,
mange sores knitting her eyebrows,
crust rimming nose holes, white chin hair,
a bloodied knee. No chatter –
her cauled eyes aimed below the sea horizon.
The driver perched on the bumper to have his coffee.
None of us talked to her.
I asked the driver, *Y su amiguita?*
Pues, mono guisa'o.
Monkey stew, bound for euthanasia.
Did she lope through city alleys or plunder peppers,
pumpkins or melons from a farmer's field?
Was she a swimmer from Cayo Santiago,
where specimens in the free-ranging colony
are tattooed with numbers,
studied by social biologists who
deliver monkey chow by motor boat every day?
I've heard that one scientist proved
that adult macaques are better at counting
apple slices than human babies
are at counting graham cracker cookies.
The behaviourists seek to know
What is fear?
How does one choose a mate?
How does one use power to overcome another?
At a party, I once met a scientist who travelled
daily to monkey island to study male aggression

in the seven bands the macaques have formed.
She told us that some funded researcher
borrowed a harpy eagle from an institution.
He wanted to know if it could be true
that harpies can carry off a small child,
so he released the eagle on Cayo Santiago.
Maybe it it grabbed a macaque and flew off into the blue,
or it returned, trained to respond to a whistle.
He unleashed an airborne agent of terror
on an island of a thousand East Indian monkeys
kept half a mile off the coast of Puerto Rico.
What *is* fear?
She was in the cage, and something
was going to happen to her.

CARDBOARD OSCARS

In his last week of presidency, Barack Obama commutes the sentence of political prisoner Oscar López Rivera (El Viejo), who is released after serving thirty-five years for "seditious conspiracy".

When Oscar arrives in Puerto Rico under house arrest, hundreds of life-size cardboard cut-out stand-up Oscars take a timeout. They have marched with their un-posable feet in hundreds of Free Oscar street protests. In a few short weeks 74-year old Oscar López Rivera will be able to walk freely in his homeland.

One cardboard Oscar dances over the hot sand in bare feet with his granddaughter at the beach Buyé de Cabo Rojo.

One cardboard Oscar joins the food scavengers' movement, gathering fruit, trading seedlings, and growing makeshift organic gardens on small plots of captured land.

One cardboard Oscar spends the day watching Monarch butterflies flying off to join the great migration.

One cardboard Oscar, despite his white hair, becomes a young university student working for $4.25 an hour under the labour reform.

One cardboard Oscar becomes a *tecato*, swaying to the clave beat at an intersection, until he is captured by cameramen of *National Geographic,* who claim that the street drug of choice, the horse tranquilizer Xylazine, is turning Puerto Rico "into a ZOMBIE NATION."

One cardboard Oscar haunts the phony offices of voted-out politicians or other *batatas* with repugnantly high salaries who are advisors to the Legislature. That cardboard Oscar gathers dust and lint, waiting for one of them to show up at work.

One cardboard Oscar walks the paths of the rainforests of el Yunque. His prison eyes adjust to the colours of allamandas, amapolas, heliconias, orchids, torch ginger lilies, red firespikes and impatiens.

One cardboard Oscar walks to el Capitolio after the new governor's public address, joining the crowd chanting down the governor's plan, Promesa, the U.S., and the coming austerity whirlwind. Protestors have carved riot shields from plastic traffic barrels.

Encapuchados beat the shields in rhythm on the road barriers set up by the police, who are now in formation on the steps of the Capitol. The crowd sings, burns a flag, and burns a man in effigy inside a silver garbage can.

MUSE

She always walks at the threshold of shadows
under the awnings of the locked car lot,
through flood lights of the war monument,
past clacking pool tables of Confetti Drink Confetti
and the unlit storefront of Iglesia el Cielo de Fuego,
late, under rain, through night, into day.

In the heat, she walks by el Cuartel de Policia,
near botánicas and kioskos of Plaza Mercado,
treading through demolished ruins of Roxy Hotel,
which once kept a carousel pony at its doorway.

White hair, worn to her shoulders,
a grim, schoolgirl face, and a decade
in the same clothes, an embroidered vest
and jeans skirt, street-dingy, pockets filled.

Like the children who pack pockets with rice
for pigeons in the Plaza de Armas, or like
my father who plugged his pockets with nuts
when my self-starved mother no longer ate meals,
this woman fills up her pockets with nubs,
the last morsel of pencils.
                              As she walks, she writes,
a notebook always in hand. *Untie me*
say the tennis shoes dangling over high wires; *firma
tu nombre en mis paredes* utters a boarded-up bank;
it's your unlucky day cries a lotto ticket booth.

She walks, and she writes. Always, I wanted
to know what station she was tuned to, what
she was observing, which frequencies of dawn
and casualties of dusk, memories of family lost,
chance happenings, or confessions filled her book.

One day in el Paseo, I almost collided with her.
She held her notebook open like a preacher
holds a Bible, and I saw the pages. Many times
and in many styles, I had imagined her handwriting!
Constricted cursive, shaky print, or slanting loops?
The pages were shiny slick with lead, written on
over and over again until letters merged into a solid
sea of pencil gloss. Not one word decipherable!

THE WOMAN YOU ARE LOOKING FOR MIGHT HAVE BEEN REMOVED, HAD HER NAME CHANGED, OR IS TEMPORARILY UNAVAILABLE

Please try the following: Click a button in your browser to find a link to me, a woman who sits at her kitchen table past midnight, Eddie Palmieri always playing on her radio.

— The coquis and pond frogs sing outside her window. *Mami told me there would be nights like this,* they sing, *when even storm clouds refuse you.*

— Sir, what are you browsing for? A Río Piedras schoolgirl in Catholic plaid miniskirt, with two jump-rope braids and white anklet socks? Midday, I meet him on the street. I ask, "Is that your daughter?" He says, "No." I say, "Is that your daughter?" He says, "I was just taking her back to school."

— You see, it takes time to brush my hair, dress in nightclothes that open like top sails, drifting me past your arms to the bay. Schoolgirls are ready — waiting for you every afternoon.

— The coquís are singing *bon voyage* songs. Adiós, little school girl in a dark tunic. The moon clock above the bank strikes el mediodía. You are there, girl, in his room above the bank in the plaza.

— So tonight, I sit up late, and I think about when I was a girl. The small town library basement was cool and dark. I stacked my books high and read in the afternoons until my father packed away his hammer and left work. My mother was sick, always sleeping or talking with spirits that rode her body endlessly.

— I loved the sea. The rough, lava-formed ledges that blocked off tidal pools. Microscopic animals in the sea water I took to school in a jar.

— Use any search engine you like. You'll never find that school girl's name.

— I am a brass bed going rusty. For I think it is a gift to have time for reading and thinking and going to school, despite the small torments of the playground.

— Look for the webpage where one school girl (is she even eleven years old?) is dividing her day by what happens before and after the white moon of that bank clock strikes noon.

— The woman you are looking for is not a woman yet.

— Sir, use a search engine like <u>Google</u> to look for information about available Puerto Rican school girls on the Internet. Short, pleated, plaid skirts rolled at the waist to make them shorter. I'm eating arroz con dulce, growing thicker at the middle. Tonight, I let my cursor blink.

.

MAN HAFFI TRY

1. Bus Terminal by Coronation Market

Later, all the way to Montego Bay,
the screen above the driver's head
will play a kungfu film in which arms
are severed in spouts and sprays of blood,
my sick friend spewing into her paper bag.

Now, pushed to the back-window seat,
waiting for the bus to fill every bench,
I can't ignore the man outside, under
my window, who is not selling grater cakes.
He sells himself, singing out his offer
in raw detail, how he can suck me,
and perform such a list of triple-X things,
teenage world-class lover, zagga zow –
I thought "Badmen nuh bow."
Women in dresses with travelling packages
turn to look at me. The youtman, immovable,
tells me for an hour all the ways
in which my pum pum ah goh feel good.

2. Walking on the Street in Liguanea

Miss, Miss, yuh fat.
Yuh fat bodder me.
Yuh fat bodder me bad.
I turn to face the man following me –
What happen, you can't carry this?
I say to him.
Yuh fat, he says.
If you don't like it, don't look,
I say.

No, no, Miss, I mean
I mean, yuh fat bodder me –
I like it. Yuh have a boyfren?

3. In the Bank on the UWI Mona Campus

Hi, there, lady, where you from?
You want to see my pistol?
The bank guard pulls his safety revolver
from its holster – frosted, ribbed barrel
pointing at me in his extended palm.
You see how it nice?
He rubs the mother-of-pearl grip
with his other hand, *Touch it,* he says.
Puerto Rico? They have beautiful women
there? Yes, the women are truly beautiful,
I say. *I mean you. You want to go out?*

4. Walking in Montego Bay

A voice behind us –
Excuse me, excuse me.
My friend keeps walking.
Miss, you have something
on your backside.
You have something.
My friend keeps walking,
but I turn. *She have something*
white on her.
I look, and it is true.
He's right, you know,
I say. It looks like chalk,
your whole bottom.
Maybe when we sat

on the stairs back there.
She always wears black silk
blouses and trousers.
She dusts off her bottom.
Thanks, I say. *Yes, I,* he says.

5. *Walking Below Sovereign*

Hey, Hollywood!

6. *In a Taxi*

The windshield sun-screen banner
of the taxi says "Wuki Duki."
Wookie Dookie? I ask,
that's the name of your car?
The driver corrects me, *Wucky Ducky.*
Wucky Ducky? What does it mean?
He laughs and doesn't want to tell me.
But, then he gives in.
*You know, it's like you work the gyal
and then duck, like not see her again,
a one-night stand, you know, wucky-ducky.*
Oh, okay, Wuki Duki.

AT THE KIOSK OF LA GITANA

Mano. Bring your two sandbags over here.
Yes, you, mi amor. Ven acá, papito.
Mira, guapo, I have something for you.
Enciende tu Lola, just what you need,
mi viejito. And I have advice for you, dear.
When you go home, sweep
and wipe all of the dust from your room.
Use a fresh mop-head and a little Mr Clean
in the water. No, not Fabuloso or Lestoil
or any of the soapy floor rinses of La Madama
and Abre Camino that I sell in my shop.
Mr Clean, the bald man with the earring,
and swab the floor well.
Horny Lion Be the Lion? Oh, yes,
this one is good, too good.
You will want this one?
My dear, you must let in fresh air,
and put clean sheets on the bed, no stains,
and take some of these lilies
to put in a glass vase by the bed.
Just a few sweet flowerstalks will do.
Hold out your hands! Ay, señor, you must trim
and file those nails well. Short and clean.
No jagged edges, me entiendes?
If the other products don't produce a result,
use my favourite, Levanta Tu Don Juan.
Take a good shower, rubbing every crevice
with mint soap. It is summer,
the season of mildew. I'm going to slip
into your bag Capsulas China Doll de Dr Ming –
She will call you Muñeco the next morning.
And listen, Papisongo, that is all that it takes.
But one more thing, think about her and take time.
Sometimes when she dreams, she wakes gasping,

short of air, still panting, with her chocha deep
muscle-aching like her little gata has been launched
into a star-birthing nebula, pummelled by meteorites,
yes, like she had been doing el perreo
with Mr Clean all night long in her dreams.
No importa si ella es una viejita;
her hamburger is gonna burn
from that kind of dream. We are all viejitas verdes,
my love, and you must transport us
to that kind of delight on your old caballo.
Kinky Spirit might be the cure,
but it's not my choice.
If all goes well, and afterwards her hair
covers the pillow, and she smiles with closed eyes,
and her face glows, say nothing. It's not you.
She's remembering how, only once,
when she was young and with a different lover,
he observed her in such a state of fulfilled pleasure
that he told her she looked just like an angel.
Look for the glow, but do not disturb her.
Think, tranquila, and lie far from her on the bed.
It is summer. It is hot. Ay, how I am sweating.
Take this last packet, Don Guapo,
for your journey to Paradise Ultra Plus.

.

THE FLYING WALLENDAS IN PUERTO RICO

Rigging under him, sea wind pushing his tank-top,
no crow's nest to climb to, no harness or net,
he is ten stories up in the air, his sky-wire tethered
between two towers of a beach-front hotel,
four-lane avenue below, where traffic stymies
in gusts blown in by lagoon mouth to lift dresses
of tourists walking to boutiques.

His breath and eyes follow this line;
the 26 bones of his foot, cased in damp naugahyde
of a slipper sewn by his mother,
settle with each step on the high-wire; ankles flex,
hips lower, body lifts in suspension,
as he edges forward, balancing pole, a long oar,
rowing him towards his mother, who approaches
from the other end of the nickel-wide wire.

From that height, his eyes won't sweep
the palm rows of Condado, or graffitied atolls
of gutted buildings in Santurce, dark rain
cloud-cover above, or even his mother's body,
as she kneels midway, sits sideways on the wire,
as if on an aerial trapeze, bends forward to touch
her breast to the cable.

He is Nik Wallenda, of the seventh generation
of Flying Wallendas, and this is the spot,
in the chute of air under the mid-point,
where his great grandfather entered
the collective memory of Puerto Rico.
He has watched the video hundreds of times.
But, now he watches the wire.

He kneels in tribute. Then, he must over-extend a leg
and leap over the length of his stooped mother,
land 26 bones on the cable, shift the weight
of his body to those bones, and wait for her to stand,
so that each may finish his crossing. She cannot do it.
She tries. In the rain-misted frame of my camera,
two hawks circle high above them.
Nik and his mother are not near to one tower
or the other. The wire buzzes. Delilah is not stable.
She can't get her feet under her. It will happen again.

Karl Wallenda, 73, is dead on the street,
having smashed into a taxi, *ventre à terre*,
at 100 miles per hour – Please, intervene
before Nik and Delilah tumble through columns of air,
three decades after Karl did.

And so, on the signal, two angels drop down
on fly wires – sleek in guayaberas
and creased pantalones, hawk wings, oiled hair,
fedoras and 70s laced-up brown-cream shoes –
to pick up Karl Wallenda by the arms,
set him upright on the slack, shillyshally
jump-rope wire, bucked by ocean winds that
are off the Beaufort scale of nautical wind speeds.

It is not good to see him dance on the live wire,
his attempt to crouch, grasp, perch,
discarded balancing pole see-sawing,
pivoting on the axis of the wire, buffeting Wallenda
into his last plunge and topple.
                              Instead, our angels reverse him.
It's 1978, but he lives, moonwalking backwards
off the wire, back into 1976, across the sky-wire
high above Veteran's Baseball Stadium,
US and colonial flags waving to the crowd below

from the ends of his balancing pole.
In 70, he moonwalks backwards across
Georgia's Tallulah Gorge, and then, he picks up
Wallendas, who had fallen and were broken
and killed, in high-wire pyramid acts.
In fuchsia boleros and bloomers, he races
backwards over Ringling Bros. and Bailey's wires,
through his winter camp in Sarasota, past
the dancers and aerialists, lovers who wanted
to knife-gouge a throat or acid-burn a pretty face
over him, past hundreds of martinis with
tiny-toothpick balancing poles piercing green olives,
until he is back in Magdeburg, Province
of Saxony, Kingdom of Prussia,
of the German Empire. It is World War I,
and he is a child, balancing on top of stacks
of chairs for tips in the Biergartens.
He is eight, and perhaps his father has already
left the family. His sister is ill. He carries her
to the hospital, but she dies in his arms.

He is four years old, and his eyes do not look
into his father's. He is a boy who has crawled
into the silent chamber of his own inner ear.
In that quiet labyrinth, where sound will never
be perceived again,
he searches for his equilibrium.
He chooses flight. A dynasty of flight,
a family earning the silence of wind
while balanced up high on the wire.
His father's hand pulls back from the hard,
violent cuff he has just delivered
to Karl's ear, the ear that will not hear
for the rest of Karl's life.

It is 1978, bring him back now, to Puerto Rico,
to his aged body, with arthritis,
double hernia, and fractured clavicle,
to the moment he knew he was free falling.
That air shaft in Condado, in the middle of the street,
between two hotel towers, belongs to Karl Wallenda,
because we remember where he took flight.

As easily as I place word after word on the blue wire
of my lined notebook, return now to Nik Wallenda
and his mother, who in her second try, stands.
They finish their steady sky walk,
and Nik tells cameramen he was never scared.
I held my breath for Delilah, one link in the chain
of the Flying Wallendas. Nik Wallenda quotes
his great grandfather, "Life is on the wire,
everything else is just waiting."

WHAT HE BROUGHT FOR ME

a verray parfit gentil knight
— Chaucer

Mighty Tiger, in scissor-frayed knee-pants,
goads the crowd with a tepid tune,
begging Parliament to honour their public duty
to society's poorlings, *cause we catching hell,*
but it's high-fête season. No cheers
for vexation this bacchanal night of prelim heats
in the packed London Calypso Tent
at Yaa Asantewaa Arts and Community Centre.

His rival ushers Tiger off-stage – no disrespect –
when the ABC Band strikes up. Lord Cloak strolls
as he sings in trim crème-coloured suit.
Ten-time champion and reigning monarch,
he is pure charisma. He sings for an end to war
in Bosnia, Rwanda and the Middle East.
We warm to his jollity and swank, his rich voice,
which says he is still a Trini, a born-Calypsonian,
a *bon vivant*. The new monarch is not yet named,
but everybody giving him back-pats and calling him *Cloak.*

We meet on a Sunday afternoon in Tavistock Gardens.
I sit on a park bench. Cloak pulls out a notebook
where he has penned lyrics for the Monarch Final,
singing me a preview of drafted bits.

'What You Bring For Me?' – he cannot fail;
the audience is bound to love this one,
for everybody who travels home to the Caribbean
must fill a grip with electronics, shirts, shoes, music,
brassieres and panties for family and friends,
and must never, never arrive with just one small bag
of their own travelling clothes. *I love them, but it's true,*
you know. When I go back home on holiday:

'What you bring for me?' I suppose if I was living there,
I might have said the same. They don't want to know
if I'm healthy, but 'what you bring?' That's why I making
that song. Brothers and sister – but they like shark.

At twenty-one, as Errol Brown, he left Trinidad
for Britain, begged a fellow to loan him a cloak
in that first rain-bone-cold summertime. West Indians
called him Cloak. The name stuck, so he added on *Lord*
for his first calypso bout in the Tent.
In Carnival season, he is Lord and often Monarch,
but at his day job, he is a squire
at White Knight Laundry, where hotels
and restaurants hire linens for special occasions.
Later, walking Notting Hill and Ladbroke Grove,
I stumble, surprised, upon this laundry
on Kensal Road – on the signboard a White Knight
in full armour, waving his spinneret flag,
mounted on his rearing white horse.

But now, I tag along to a pub, for a rendezvous
with Cloak's best pal, a Trini who is with
his Irish matey, a red-haired gal, who likes bold jokes,
long drinks and thigh-smacking laughs.
They invite us to the friend's flat.
He has a grand reel-to-reel audiotape player,
spools of Lord Cloak's calypsos, and cartons
of Carib beer stacked under the stairwell.
The friend brings out a big calabash
full of Carib to share. *This is how we used to drink*
at home. Lord Cloak sings along with the reels,
recounting until six in the morning
his days in the Grove. I lurch to my bed-sit,
but he must greet the White Knight at eight.

At the Monarch Final, he slays the Mighty Tiger
and all other pretenders. On Carnival day,

I run into Cloak near the Westway Flyover.
Wait! he tells me. *Wait right here, I have something*
for you! My apartment is close by. Wait now, I coming back.
Twenty minutes later, I see him chipping through
police barricades and mas' bands. *This is Carnival!*
You must have a flag, eh? You must wave a flag
in the air! He ceremoniously hands me
a sealed plastic bag. It contains a pre-moistened
white terry-cloth washcloth folded, tightly rolled,
the kind that might be warmed and handed
steaming hot to a patron in some posh restaurant –
now a carnival flag, courtesy of the King – a warm
and simple act of bachelor noblesse he shares with me.

He invites me to join him for a lime in the forecourt
of his friend's apartment, but I want to walk
to see all the bands, and look out for friends
on the lorries of the mobile sound systems
and steel pan bands. I am leaving London for the islands,
penniless, after two years here. Next to me,
he watches a few bands, and then, with a nod,
disappears back into the soca multitudes.
All day, I jump and wave my flag, waving goodbye.

Mr. Brown, it has been twenty years now since
that day. We not getting young, sir. I see
that the Mighty Tiger passed. From Puerto Rico,
I surf to see how you getting on over there in cold England.
In an internet video of a recent Monarch Final at Tabernacle,
you sport a dapper brown bowler hat and a brown dandy suit –
crowned thirteen times, you say the youngsters
coming up now in the Tent are cutting your ass.
It's good to see you singing, *bon vivant.*
I want to thank you, Cloak.
How's your health? You healthy? What a ting you do
for me, eh? What an amazing thing –
that flag you bring for me.

69

REVEL REBEL
for M.L.R.

Mounted constables of the Met
trot tall war-horses about the road,
calling out on bullhorns
for revellers to leave the area,
but we huddle into clusters on the street.
A cone of helicopter light sweeps
up Notting Hill and the Grove.

Martina and I sit on a low wall,
sharing curried roti and rice,
our bruised feet bare and draggling.
It's late on Great Western Road,
hours after the police curfew.
We have been asked to head home,
but we haven't moved.

Something starts happening up the street,
police crews blocking off streets
to corral us…? No, they are throwing
barricades and road blocks out of the way,
running to stay ahead of the disturbance.
Push back, fall back, a commotion,
coming through, coming right through.

We can't see the cause,
but people
surge from nowhere,
dancing up the midnight road.
We hear it now, no soca beat
or steel pan, but thunder decibels
of the bass pumping up
Buju Banton's ragga growl,
a sound system lorry blaring
like a cruise ship's horn.

On the move this late? Mas' finished
long time, but the truck busts the hurdles,
storming Portobello, Tavistock and the Great Western,
driving the wrong way,
against the official map
of the Carnival route.
"I could go on and on,
the full has never been told"—

It's Michael! Martina and I scramble,
jogging over to the sound truck
of People's War Carnival Band.
Michael, original mas' rebel,
wining hips next to massive speakers.

We reach up to shake his hand,
bumping along with his band
in j'ouvert costumes,
How the West was Won cowboys,
Devils in Blue policemen,
Palmares maroons of Brazil's Quilombos.

Heroes of the Wild, Wild West,
Nat Love –
Dead-Eyed Dick, Stage-Coach Mary,
Beckwourth of the Crow Nation,
the Buffalo Soldiers, all dancing
with baton-gripping blue bobbies,
costumed like those who killed
Joy Gardner and Brian Douglass,
Mas' makers damning a seven o'clock curfew.
Road mek fe walk on Carnival day.

We had looked for People's War all day –
Martina and I had felt let-down,
until we heard that lorry plowing

the police right out of the road,
Michael's force on the move,
rumbling past the fake-fake natty beach shacks
of Coca Cola's tropical soda "Lilt"
and through gentrified walk-ups of Notting Hill –
Michael's ragamuffin tank.

No constable tries to stop
this Pied Piper leading us
out of Ladbroke Grove,
showing the mounted police
on their dancing horses
something about public order
and crowd control.

PULSE

Orlando, the magic kingdom
where the gunman mowed us down.
— Andre Bagoo

We carry the names of those
we have lost as incantations.
— Vicente Cervantes

PULSE. What we have. What they do not have.

It was family night at the prom with my daughter.
Parents pay for seven years to a collective fund
so that their teenagers' senior prom is a grand hotel affair
that lasts for three days of dressing up, dancing,
and rule breaking. Her dress was sewn by a madam
of haute couture in San Juan. She hadn't sewn African fabric
for a prom dress. She called us to many fittings.
The fabric was patterned with flying birds, swallows
or swifts. My daughter wore a wreathe of flowers.
Students and wildly embarrassing mothers, mainly,
danced to a live band, playing Latin rhythms, cumbia,
boleros, salsa, merengue, reggaetón, and some rock.
They danced until their dresses and dress shirts were sweaty.

PULSE. The rhythms of Latin music that make us feel happy.

No gunman brought an automatic assault rifle into the hotel
to bloody and wound and kill all our children
while they danced. But words began to hum around
the ballroom. Orlando. Pulse. Latin music night. LGBT.
The moment I heard, I knew. Without numbers.
Without names. Without newsreel faces. Forty-nine dead.
All vital. Now erased. Half of them, ours. Orlando
is the Promised Land. Island children are fed Disney dreams.

73

Everyone has family there who can get you free passes to the park.
It is the arrival zone for Puerto Ricans migrating with families
or needing to leave their parents behind. I looked at the faces
of our dear ones on the dance floor – my daughter celebrating
herself and friends who are bi-curious, gay, lesbian, non-binary, trans.
Only slightly younger versions of the massacred clubbers
in Orlando, elated, dancing, alive, in front of me.
The queer writers I have mentored, my students, so many
had left for Florida. Were they there, at Pulse, when the gunman
obliterated and maimed our children? Each face
that later appeared in the media seemed familiar.
Then, they started bringing bodies
to the island for funerals in Ponce, Caguas, Guánica, Río Grande.

PULSE. A club you would want to go to on Latin night.

The nurse who was supposed to start a doctoral program
was carried in a glass carriage, drawn by a team of horses.
Etc., etc.

PULSE: Echoic memory,
Harmonic motion, bassline.

I told my girl about the men whom I have loved, *the woman.*

PULSE: María arrived ready to rumba, to rave
Storm that carried my island girl away.

PULSE: Breath, incantation, names we carry.

One year later, a mother in Río Grande walks
around her son's room every day. A father tattoos
the face of his son over his heart. What balm
can we offer?
                My girl messages me, safe,
for now, but not here, there, clubbing, dancing

74

over there, with the Puerto Rican and dominicano students
until the wooden floor nearly collapses, laughing,
sandwiched by women, who give her their numbers.

PULSE: Rhythms of music that make us feel happy.

Here, the government tries to ditch
same sex marriage. The Church is still the Church,
and PATOPHOBIA LIVES. My girl messages me
about her loves. Children not yet killed by guns
march everywhere.

MEMOIR OF REPAIRS TO THE COLONY

CENTRING THE GALAXY FROM COROZAL

Blue-dust nebula of Orion's belt
and two bright stars, glowing Venus,
and, above her, tiny Mars, found here
in Corozal, on a hill of Cibuco, behind
a plantation house, where the guaraguao glides
over us, and amateur astronomers
sketch with green laser-pointers
Cassiopeia, Pollux, and the Seven Sisters
Taínos planted their crops by.
These 'scopes are modern,
guided to programmed coordinates.
The centrepiece is missing, though.
The middle of the field is empty,
where once a month, for thirty years,
Don Gregorio unpacked crates,
and climbed a stepladder to build,
section by section, his monumental
telescope, black cylinders like wide stovepipe
joints, with refractors and large bevelled,
ground-glass lens that he adjusted
by hand throughout the night,
equipped only with a star chart, a red penlight,
and his own sense of how celestial bodies
shift between dusk and dawn.
Years ago, I saw Jupiter and Saturn
through his 'scope, learned from him how
to look into the heart of the universe
through the teapot stars of Sagittarius
and call that haze the Vía Láctea.
When the planetarium at the science park
broke down, and no funds were found
to fix it, Don Gregorio still organized
public lectures there. He had a dream
and some donated land in the hills of Corozal,

where he wanted to build a grand solarium
so children could come on excursions
to view the sun. He worked with NASA on his plans,
convinced the mayor of the pueblo,
and the island legislature allocated funds.
But elections came, the government changed,
and the project fell. I called him at home once.
As it happened, his wife had died (cancer took her quickly)
and I was a woman's voice on the phone.
He told me about his wife,
and that damned bird, a blue pigeon
his wife had rescued, a dirty bird
always under foot. He'd never liked it
walking freely about the house.
After his wife died, it fell to him to feed it.
The day of my call, the bird had escaped
the screened-in porch, standing
dumbly behind his car tire. He had backed
over it, of course. He didn't know why he
was telling me about it. He died
in the recent season of the super moon,
a celestial event that will not occur again
in my lifetime. I sat that night on my front stairs
viewing the lakes and seas of the moon
through the binoculars that Gregorio
had recommended years back.
I didn't know then that he had passed.
Tonight, the hill of Cibuco is full of families,
and the sky that earlier was bright with stars
is blanked out in cloud-cover.
When I ask, the young astronomy professor
says that this is the Society's first observation
since Don Gregorio's death. He points
to the bare centre of the field. *Su telescopio
siempre estaba ahí,* he says. *Right there.*

NARANJITO

Abu, dozing in a satin chemise,
drifting away in a hammock
knotted to her balcony, dissolves
back into the green mountain.
Her dreams quilt a hillside
into a patchwork façade of green houses.
Homes cataract from high slopes down to Río de la Plata.
Re-painted jade, lime, mint, green papaya,
sea-washed glass, brightest green of iguanas.
Camouflaged, each house dematerializes.

On the green checkerboard of the basketball court,
teens, playing keep-away, jump for a last
inside hand lay-up and then swallow
themselves down into the green of beer bottles.
Skateboarders back-side grind on green ramps,
sailing up three green flights of staircases.

A van selling mazorcas, pastelitos
and budín de pan fades into a green ravine,
its bullhorn song subsiding.

It's quiet now on the mountain.
In his green kareoque bar, Vicente holds
an open jar to one ear and hears
weather patterns, clouds walking the high ridges,
no grind of industry or clamour of metal,
just mist and things sprouting,
underworld water filtering through karst.

Even the painters who wear fatigues and splash
rollers into their great buckets of green, finally paint
themselves into the upstairs corners of the grand houses
of scions of coffee barons and the small casitas
of children of coffee pickers. They vanish.

In El Cerro de Naranjito, a pueblo built by coffee,
an aroma of drying and roasting beans,
coffee highs and delirium tremens did not drive
architects to make even one flourish, one frilled
cornice or fluted balustrade. Each pueblo
of this isle has its postcard plaza and cathedral,
a line of Seville orange trees where men and women
whisper piropos de amor, promises scented by blossoms,
haloed by bees, but not here in Naranjito.

A range of mountains cradles box row buildings,
the ugly gauntlet of this town.

Workers of the cafetales dreamed of endurance
until Hurricane San Felipe uprooted their lives.
Paint it all back into the mountainside.

En la montaña, in a green maroonage,
families gather at the community centre
to remake the pueblo in their image,
to find the cemí of these mountains.

At just the right angle, in just the right light,
the hill looks pixelated. Green monk parakeets
fly into green walls, bruising wings and dropping feathers.

Sometimes artefacts are found by visitors
looking for Naranjito, a rusted sewing-machine needle,
a few Goya cans of petit pois,
a framed portrait of a mother's lost son,
a quiet radio singing,
Vámonos pa'l monte, vámonos pa' allá.

CHAIRMAN OF THE COMMITTEE ON NOMENCLATURE

By bel canto, coo, hoot, pip, or trill,
young Leopold could name that bird,
using string to noose wrens and warblers,
bag up his feathery collection for display.
Little deaths, eroto-executions, sado-scientific
quest to document through snuffing out
winged things with chloroform, stirred
a quick ache in Nathan Leopold, but no remorse.
Split the throat that sings. He discovered
that to classify, study, order, name was a thrill.
Birding wasn't his only passion after he met
Richard Loeb. They wanted to be brilliant,
to be ubermen of their generation,
to have coverage by the press,
to control the pulse of another's life,
to carry it off as planned, to get off scot-free,
to nurse a secret thrill that only they shared,
a kind of endless orgasm of the imagination.
They planned a perfect murder.
They nabbed a school boy who was walking home.
Things didn't go as planned. When he could not be
chloroformed as easily as a bird, they hammered his head
inside the car, and then lugged the broken Bobby Franks
to Leopold's birding field and stuffed him into a storm drain,
dropping Leopold's glasses from a shirt pocket.
Loeb died in jail, while Leopold was used
as a malaria lab rat at Statesville Pen.
A priest bartered his release, so he flew to Puerto Rico,
a bird of passage, an assassin turned ornithologist,
who would write the definitive book on Puerto Rican birds.
Re-making himself, but keeping Loeb's photo on his bedstand,
he re-named our endemic birds and transients,
those that return in the fall or spring,
but do not breed or live here year around.

The island's way of doing things frustrated him.
For instance, the maze of Spanish names
for the Puerto Rican tody, which, by the way,
generally kept itself from being seen.
When Leopold asked what we call the bird,
la gente sang out so many names: "Medio Peso",
"San Pedrito", "San Pedro", "Peseta", "Papagayo",
"Barracolino", "Verador", and "Verdadón".
You see, Puerto Rican birds resist attempts
to name them just one thing. They don't reply
or come when called by any of their names.
And so Nathan Leopold, Jr., specialised
in the plain pigeon, la paloma sabanera
de Puerto Rico, *Columba inornata wetmorei*,
Bird #116 on his checklist.
He found ten near Cidra in October of 1963.
In November, he collected a male specimen,
illustrated on page 119 of his bird book,
wings splayed.
Coo-coo-booyah.

MEMOIR OF REPAIRS TO THE COLONY

At Isla de Cabras,
      the sea licks pockmarks
         and jagged spires
    into the rocks so that no one
can climb down to the tidal pools. Pebbles
      and crockery shards mark
a path along the ridge to the ruins.
      A strange spongy grass grows
over the hill and inside the two roofless
      rooms of brick, mortar and stone.
One for men, another for women,
both left uninhabitable by hurricanes in 1916.

      If one stands in the doorway
   of the women's quarters,
      looking across the water, past
the deep-sea trench, to the castle fortress
of el San Felipe del Morro,
      then the cemetery
         is down a slope on the right.
Its picket fence is gone. Graves are unmarked,
but I believe there are many.

Leprosarium, such a botanical word,
like *lepidoptera* and *mariposario* –
like the name of a rarity in a Victorian temperate
glasshouse of mallows, rushes, saltbush,
   and butterflies darting over the sedge.

Leprocomio Insular, to insulate
colonial guards, Spanish, then American,
      from infected masses.
They were built on the big island,
     and then on this islet, off the north coast,

constantly whipped by wind,
        high sea-spray and salt mist that seeped
and burned into all bloody crevices of wounds.

    Those leper paupers, sequestered here,
lived under the sun like desert saints,
        in an abandoned quarantine station.
They made a garden that didn't thrive.
            The well lacked fresh water.
They had a coal-pot kitchen stocked
by the weekly boat that brought a priest-doctor
with salves of arsenic and creosoted cod-liver oil,
glass bottles of El Rey Dolor, thick,
yellow chaulmoogra oil distilled by steam, suspended
        in an emulsion of gum and camphor.
            Once a week, El Rey Dolor
was injected intramuscularly or subcutaneously,
causing panic in the patients;
lepers swelled and burned in fever
with every hypodermic.

The Protestants sent a handyman to make repairs.
    He carried a baseball in his pocket,
to play toss with nine-year-old Eleutorio.
    When the handyman rowed away
Eleutorio stood in the line of patients
waving goodbye to him with a hat.
    When the handyman got leprosy,
        he, too, was confined to the island.

For ten years after hurricanes blew the roof out,
        lepers were still kept on this rock.
    The handyman built coffins,
                one for Eleutorio.
In 1926, patients were transferred
from Isla de Cabras to a new hospital colony

in Trujillo Alto, managed by child-murderer
    Nathan Leopold, who published scientific papers
        on our lepers.

I swam once at Isla de Cabras.
    A brown oily-smudge stayed stinking
        on my skin for more than a week.
The island is now a police shooting-range.
        A No Swimming sign is posted.
          The water, itself is sick, laden
        with arsenic, cadmium, chromium, cyanide,
pathogens, and pesticides that penetrate skin.

VIEQUES, 1961
The filming of *The Lord of the Flies*

Bombed
by robber flies,
Simon squatted,
observing
the buzzed-out,
rheumy eyes
of a spiked
pig's head.

I can't hardly move
with those creeper things,
Piggy said.

At the mountaintop,
a puppet paratrooper
drooped and nodded
as tree limbs pulled
his strings.

The island
was tropical,
but not deserted —
not then, not yet,
though a covert plan
had been drawn up
to relocate 8,000
fishing villagers,
cane workers,
to dig up
their dead;
yes, to make even
the dead turn refugee,
migrate on a ferry,

to crate and replant
their tombstones
on the mother island.

Woolworth's
Woolnor Corp.
wanted the south coast
to build a golf course, marina
and 100-bed hotel.

US Navy owned the fly-space
of la Isla Nena,
had a sixty-bed hospital
for marine emergencies –
wanted no tourists
swarming up on beaches,
sand flies
in the season
of amphibious exercises.

We found an island
off the coast of Puerto Rico.
A jungle paradise;
miles of palm-fringed
beaches owned by Woolworth's.
They lent us the island
in exchange for a screen credit.

No evacuees of bombardiers' air-raids,
a brigade of thirty-three
young British boys
arrived on planes
that didn't crash.
Three of the boy
actors were Puerto Rican,
and 'Ralph', (who confused
the pink-lipped song

of the conch shell
with male prerogative,
and power), was from
an army camp in Jamaica.

Near Esperanza and Sun Bay,
they barracked for three months
in a ruined pineapple plant –
an army cot for each boy.

Jeeps, trucks, tanks,
recoiless rifles, bazookas,
mortars, mines, missiles,
conventional and guided,
that would later leave
the surfaces of the island test-sites lunar –
the boys had none of these,
just one knife and sharpened branches,
for hunting wild pigs
and each other. But the
weapons were there, in the bunkers
beyond the camera's pan.

Maybe there is a beast,
Simon suggested.

In April, director Brook began to shoot
in black and white
the trumpet processional along the beach,
the boys still in their school togs
crawling over a low-swung
coco palm at Media Luna; he was forced
to pause during the first week
for an incoming tally of casualties and losses
of lives, ghost ships, and sanitised
planes of Operation Pluto, a.k.a.
Operation Zapata.

The air-lifted,
groaning bodies of Cuban exilios
and US operatives filled beds
of the naval hospital in Vieques.
War wounds bloomed tropically
at the Bahia de Cochinos –
the botched invasion of the Bay of Pigs,
at la Playa de Girón,
where flies foretasted
the mingling blood of Cubans and Cubans
that wetted heads, arms, legs, and torsos.

PHOTO CAPTION: Prime Minister Fidel Castro
jumps down from a tank, as he leads
The Cuban Revolutionary Forces.

The boys played with lizards,
swam in the sea, smoked some
kind of leaves, held hermit crab races,
and chanted *Kill the pig! Slit its throat!*
when they killed Simon and set his body afloat.

They tormented 'Piggy'– *They're going
to drop a stone on you. That scene
on the schedule, Piggy's death,
it's for real. They don't need you anymore.*

When the boy actors had gone tribal enough for Brook,
they were packed off to their adults,
to their sensible parents.
They grew up.

La Isla Nena, theatre
for ceaseless rehearsals
of assaults and invasions –
school bells drowned out

by daytime live-ammo bombardments –
later ousted la Marina
after being the launch pad
for deployments to Guatemala,
Cuba, la República Dominicana,
Grenada, Haiti, the Balkans, Iraq
and Somalia.

EN EL CEMENTERIO BÚSQUEDA

> My father was buried in one of the rainiest
> cemeteries in the world.
> — Pablo Neruda

Off the marginal road of Isla Verde,
the graveyard fills with rainwater.
In the empty restaurant next door,
the down-turned glasses above the bar
take up a collection of dust.
The dark carpet smells of mildew
from damp cement floors
absorbing water run-off
from the field of cadavers.

A dead hotel by the restaurant
hosts only local clientele, a few prostitutes
who sit poolside in their négligées,
while in the courtyard, strung
with cords of randomly lit bulbs,
dry leaves bury a trashed chair-swing.
A police car is parked in the lot,
but the rooms have no guests.

It is the rainy season when aquifers fill,
underground rivers overflow,
the ground is saturated, and coastal roads
are inundated, until everyone must wade
up to their waists in flood waters
and abandon their stalled cars.

Why are there so many cemeteries by the sea,
walled-off from tourists, but there
reminding them that after the sun, buoyancy and frolicking,
everyone will end up there?

When streets flood, caskets float in the graves.
The rising water and the floaters lift and push aside
the heavy cement slabs meant to keep the dead down.
Coffins emerge and set sail. Those in the coffins
are all virgins again, interred in their stockings
and fine suits. Their testicles and vaginas
are no longer plump and pretty. They cannot be
intoxicated, except by their own fermentation.
They are less than dead now. They own
not even their monotonous headstones
washed by rain, or the lots arranged
like rows of cots in a military barrack yard.

The indignity of being a floater –
in a flotilla of coffins putting out to sea.
In their unlit cabins of their small boats,
they cannot find the shore nor see the sky.
Each grave hole with its little naufragio –
its shipwreck. The coffins escape from
the ground, but the dead, having a second
death by drowning, cannot announce,
I am here. I was. I lived. If they could,
they would fill their graves with tears.

The restaurant smells
like the absence of flowers. The hotel
smells like a fever. Call the working women
to bring their chaise lounges here
to sit by the new pools and open grasses.
My friend Mark is buried here.
At least his grave is not yet capsized.

CAMPEONATO DE TRUJILLO ALTO

At the competition corral,
in the front bleacher at the rail,
I lose the children's sounds, the crowd.
White-grey dappled Paso Fino,
smoke gathered in a brandy glass
on her stockings and hindquarters,
arched neck high-carriaged, no head toss,
her big, deep eyes concentrating,
utterly alert and focused
on the motions of the fino.
Long forelock parted, white lashes —
she does not care about her mane
or lifted tail whisking the ground.
In depths of her chest, heart hammers.
Propulsion churns from quadriceps.
Legs lift en cuatro tiempos
laterales — the one raza
with this fine isochronous gait.
Front legs fully collect, high-knee,
in short-stride, precise, rapid prance,
smooth, poco translación, no bounce,
hardly moving forward at all,
deft, inching, deliberate steps,
hooves hitting the ground with a speed
of ten beats per second. Pistons;
a fast sewing-machine needle.

I see the gaskins and cannons,
pectorals, shoulders, back, barrel,
croup, loins, flanks, strong rump, all contained,
straining in unison, no signs
of heat stress, no frothing white foam
slathering shoulders and withers,
which means the horse is done, sent out

95

to cool off. Nostrils dilated,
una perfeccionista,
she takes all the time in the world
to move past me, a touch away,
in her proud quick-step, stylish march.

She needs no movement of the reins
from her jínete, who seems to glide
rather than ride on a horse back.
He sits relaxed, no rigid spine,
in simple equestrian dress
of white shirt, black ribbon bow-tie,
small-brimmed, flat, black hat,
no use of crops or steel boot spurs.

In the corner of the corral,
he pulls the reins with one finger
to back her up, under manners,
spirited head still, ears erect,
no swishing of the tail, still high.

In front of the judges' table,
a narrow, wooden sounding board,
is in the centre of the rink,
like a fashion-model's catwalk.
The plywood plank amplifies sound,
the meter of staccato beats.

She approaches it, tracking straight
down the sounding board – los cascos
tocan, and the arena fills
with jolting reverberations –
an accurate rap of hoofbeats –
taps entering us like shrapnel,
ta-ca ta-ca ta-ca ta-ca.
Her long face is at attention,

her body, rousing athlete,
working, taxed, but maintaining grace;
hooves set down micro-distances
in front of their last locations.
This is the Classic Fino.
For years, I will think about her,
her extreme determination.

All those random Saturday drives
en el campo, las montañas
of Aguas Buenas, Guavate,
where bareback, barefooted boys trot
their Pasos at curving road's edge;

in fiestas of Loíza,
when a Santiago statue,
festooned, is paraded through streets –
Santiago, saviour of Spain,
defeater of retreating Moors,
always on horseback, a Moor's head,
decapitated, crushed under,
his stallion's triumphant front hoof –
carted through Afro-boricua
pueblo, where groups of teenage boys
pedal bicycles, trick bikes,
while dreadlocked youths canter horses;

white Paso Fino performing
the Levade and Pesade
for tourists in the Ballajá,
crimped mane in blue spotlight, dancing
with a blanquita – pale woman
in a starched, lacy bomba dress;

those black chestnut Paso Finos
riot police rode on campus,

in black tack, uniforms and shields,
truncheon-armed against students;
those Paso Finos, I have known.

Paso Fino, still in my dreams,
bred of Spanish Barb and Jennet,
the Andalusian, brought here
to Borinquen by Columbus
and Gov. Juan Ponce de León.
The conquistadors had the time
for volley, retreat and trampling
people to death on plantations
and in narrow, blue-cobbled streets
of Old San Juan – five hundred years.

White-ash pony of my daydreams –
how hard you have strained and struggled.
I want to ask you if you could
give up this training, break away
from this arena and your sport?
Rear up, strike quick, at this late date,
unseat your jínete, topple
the trainers, clench bit in your teeth?
When, if not now, would you do it?

RICANTATIONS

Hurricane María wheeled over the sea,
a day away from upending and crushing cars,
prying roofs, plucking up electrical poles,
cracking trees to the stub,
flooding plantain fields of Yabucoa.

Our avocado trees, roots rumbling,
threw down their green pears all at once,
so that when they were broken and uptorn,
their stones would tap into soil.

Blue macaws flew loudly up-mountain;
unprepared for what came, we bunkered down.

At the storm's transit from tropical to Cat 5,
I saw through louvred bedroom window,
an enormous old iguana, 5 or 6 feet
from nose to tail. He sat at the top corner
of my vine-covered fence,
bowing down chain-link with his weight.
His armour-plated face, rain-doused,
pointed into the wind. Spikes ridging his back
and black-striped tail, his orange neck flap
and haunches showed his age. In his heavy-lidded
green eyes, what knowledge? I was in the cabin
of a ship, and he was both captain and figurehead,
an ancient dragon sailing us into a sky bomb.

Boombox María, with her twisted dance track
of everything shattered, buckled and airborne,
sucked windows flapping, hammered house corners,
cisterns, fences and iron gates free-flying, hilltop
homes mud-sliding. Whatever African tulips she left
were bark-stripped, naked as bone, wind-burned.

When neighbours cleared trees and debris,
we went out onto the swamped streets.
Ceiba trees' massive trunks pulled up like radishes.
Piñones erased by sand, beach huts gone.
Signs and stop-lights curled wreckage –
Cemetery wall strewn along the hotel strip.

Young iguanas, ousted from shorn treetops,
ran into the road and were run over.
Honey bees flew into our homes,
their hives and colonies carried away,
surviving plants disrobed of flowers and fruit.
Bats whisked overhead at twilight.

Families with no roofs slept on sodden couches,
in bathrooms, on patios, in leaking garages.
National Guardsmen patrolled gas pumps,
directed traffic with their long rifles
and, guns in hand, gave out shoeboxes
of Doritos, raisins, Vienna sausages
and Coca Cola to mothers in Barrio Obrero
with kids on their hips, who had waded
through deep black water.

I fed honey bees, soaked napkins with sugar-water
and waggled the wet flags at them until
they surrendered and sipped to their fill.
But, I searched in vain for pure water
to bring to my diabetic daughter,
could invent no cooler for her insulin vials.
My ulcerated legs dripped sap and pus.
Doctors vanished. I let my daughter go
into safe exile, *charitably* evacuated.

With Carmen, Enid and Margarita, I traded
food, solar lights, and small bags of ice.

We bathed in bowls and hand-washed clothes
with tainted water, the dam at Comerío clogged
with animal carcasses, the raw sewage of Caguas
backwashing into our incoming water lines.

Eleven cargo truck containers stacked
with human corpses piled up in the coroner's back lot.

A friend found dazed bats crumpled on the ground.
She gathered them, ornaments that she hooked
by thumb claw and toes onto bare branches
of a fruit tree. In the morning, though,
like shrunken, dried mangoes, brown mounds
of the dead bats lay beneath the tree
that couldn't feed them.

A friend was hit on the head at a twilight gas station;
at another gasolinera, a woman saved her baby
from carjackers, who burned off in her car,
but spared her love.

Nothing now is normal
though remaining trees rush to green up
and flower, dogs bark, and the sea still
waves its bacterial flag over the shores.
I hear quarrelling macaws and parakeets.
Ay Le Lo Lai songs move us,
but not to full tenderness.

Still, we feel new incantations of something
primal in us, allied by our hurricane grief,
disordered, but sentient of how we are related, neighbours,
iguanas, honey bees, bats, birds, trees, islands.
What is possible now? Can we do some things
differently now?

ART BRUT

ART BRUT

I.

Thrown out of olive groves by his father,
Baldassare Forestiere travelled with the idea
of growing citrus. A new arrival, he bought
hardpan, rocky land that could never prosper
in a valley burned by summer sun,
soil-cracked by drought, fog-swamped
in winter. He survived by levelling
other farmers' tracts and grafting fruit trees.
To escape the heat, he'd go underground,
one scoop of dirt at a time, dreaming
of catacomb passages, a cool alcove,
a snug bedroom, a garden view lit with skylights.
In a cavern, eight – twelve – metres below,
he would grow wonder trees, one citrus
bearing eight kinds of fruit. He would treat
some woman, *wife*, to cedrons,
navel oranges, Valencias, tangerines, grapefruits,
and sweet lemons, while she bathed
in his hand-carved tub. In brick planters,
pear trees would thrive, pomegranates, almonds,
mulberries, palm dates, persimmons, and strawberries,
red grapes and green, rosemary, myrtle –
his fish pond stocked with fish caught
in the San Joaquin River, his own brand
of wine hand-pressed – Sangre di Christo.
All of this came to pass after forty years
of burrowing. He hand-scraped dirt, dredged
scrabble, strained his back with wheelbarrow loads
to sculpt the earth into subterranean baths,
gardens and grottos – one hundred chambers
excavated with hand tools, picks, a shovel
and sometimes a mule to move bigger rocks –

to remake the lower world into his own image.
But the woman did not want to play Persephone;
she would only have him above ground.
She could not see the charm
of his spliced trees, the sweet globes
of fruit glowing in sun shafts
of his cavernous honeycomb.

He stayed alone. Ten acres of an ant colony,
piazzas in deep vaults, meeting halls,
a space for a restaurant and dancing —
he imagined a peopled resort,
where others could see in the braced ceilings
and clay-tiled patios who Baldassare Forestiere
was, a man with little money, who'd sculpted
himself and propagated a wonder tree
still growing a bounty seventy years after his death.

I have walked down into the Earth, descended
into Forestiere's gardens, imagining his evenings,
reading alone in his small bedroom, (for he liked to read),
sitting next to the starlit skylight to tune the radio,
lifting a tired arm to put a strawberry in his mouth.

II.

Maybe I'll go to the sky,
Sabato said after his wife left
and he tired of swimming
in wine bottles. He walked
the railway lines to gather cast-off
rebar, rods he webbed
into a steel latticework of spindles
and steeples, scalloped cones,
and ribbed tetrahedrons.
He climbed higher daily.

Like a boy pulling himself up
level after level of a rocketship
jungle-gym in an abandoned park,
he climbed inside his airy cages.
He knitted gridiron, wrapping spines
in wire mesh, trowelling on cement,
embellishing with shells, florid china teacups,
blue willow plates, toy cars, mirrors,
cobalt shards of Milk of Magnesia
bottles and porcelain figurines.
After three decades, his lace towers
reached the clouds. Thirty meters up,
he intertwined needletops with arched bridges,
narrower than the width of his foot.
He traversed his scaffold without hand-rails,
grown used to misted views of Watts.
He invited all to visit Nuestro Pueblo,
and neighbours came to trace pottery chunks
in the walls and roofless doorways,
to look up, to feel it with their hands.
Sabato Rodia embedded himself into all crevices
of his lifework. Earthquakes and riots
could not pull it down.

I have put my hand
on his walls, seen the patchwork curios.
What if I used my one life
to construct these stony geometries
with only hands and thrown-out scraps?
Keep faith, Sabato, in the beauty
of delightful dream spires.

III.

Reinaldo Rios' OVNI hunters film
shaky videos, tracking aliens

through a snarl of vines and plantains
in night yards of Lajas, where a woman
believes she was abducted into the surgical room
of a spaceship, returning to Earth with scrambled intestines.
The rainforests of El Yunque hide secret labs
where the US military examines extraterrestrials
and creates genetic mutants that sometimes escape.
In an island of alien invasions, Roberto's vision
began with ink doodles on lunchtime napkins,
sent as love missives to his novia in high school.
He wrote his contract to her on tissue wisps,
ink-carved with flying saucer designs of the home
he would one day put her in. She crumpled his banners
of love and ran, as women do, when placed upon an altar
that portends a man's nebulous inner journey. He studied
industrial and fine arts – tending his love wound –
taught, saved, borrowed, retired, still intent on crafting
his napkin blueprints into a hillside glory
where he could sit, gazing down onto traffic –
the centre of his own universe.
My headlights, just two more dots in the light stream
wending homeward by Juana Díaz,
on the south coast, where near the sea,
the highway cuts through Peñoncillo,
I see the flying saucer touched down on a green hill.
Roberto's three-tier saucer, constructed of panels
of shining blue float glass – that blue of Chagall's stained glass,
coloured landing lights around the base,
flashing silver dome, lights up the hill,
dazzling the sea behind it, slowing tired motorists.
For forty years he planned and built for seven,
raiding the auto-junkers and dollar stores,
crafting each element of inside and out,
hundreds of cheap silver ashtrays welded
on the top tower; red and yellow plastic salad bowls
capping the bright running lights.

Inside, floating furniture is fastened to walls,
a table built from a chromed exhaust manifold
and auto glass, his paintings of planets
and one weeping rose. Roberto Sánchez Rivera
sits outside on the upper deck of his saucer,
where he has placed a plaster alien that raises a hand
to point at the horizon, like our Ponce de León
statues in public plazas. I see Roberto
in his boxer shorts with a bucket of iced Medallas.
He's not moping over Stella, that high-school beauty,
or staring forlornly out at some far exoplanet
revolving around a stellar corpse.
He's in the moon-glow of tonight's dance,
where he met someone and handed her a napkin
twirled into a rose. He thinks of adding
more whoomp to his saucer, maybe a gyromotor,
a liquid hydrogen something,
a magneto plásmico engine, a clutch.
He'll scoop a fist of earth,
bend one rod of rebar at a time, grab
one handful of stars; he will bring order to chaos
and funnel himself into his creation. He amazes
us with his vessel, zooming to celestial lift-off,
before some other cabrones colonise space.

OSAIN

Its tap root spears him,
red mangrove seedling,
brown-tipped arrow point,
fletching, a tuft of leaves,
like a dart it pierces him,
falling into his soul.

His paintbrush sprouts aerial roots,
so he paints the salt flats,
swamp soup of the mangroves,
arching stilt roots,
around the walls of his studio.

Rhizomes of mangrove trees, antennae
between sky and Earth, ground him,
transmit el espíritu del bosque.
This work takes him over for years.
He models grey clay to summon Osain,
to fly forward into the mangrove future
of the ancestral past of his pueblo Loíza,
Loíza Aldea. Osain runs, not like a runaway
but like a sprinting messenger,
leaning far forward, pumping
his veined arms, stretching
towards some evasive finishing line.
His urgent legs morph into tall,
churning stilts, footstalks lengthening
into the back legs of a gazelle,
hocked, calcaneus bones jutting
backwards as he springs forward.

Bark scales up the runner's ankles.
Prop roots pop out of his burning calves.
The moving man is still running.

His heart and liver shrink,
so that he can run faster.

    From matter to spirit
    is to see something beyond the senses.
    Like a tree that branches
    one sacrifices everything
    for the images that come
    and are projected.

The clay man runs;
his arboreal fingertips
flame out into waxy leaf-sprouts.
Birds sing! He sings
in the voice of a bird.

    Behind every work
    there are many emotions.
    The dilemma, the challenge
    towards a final product.
    Life is lived for lonely work;
    it cannot be avoided.

Notched face, African face,
clear-cut, whole-hearted face,
tree knot on forehead,
like Osain's one eye.
A bomba drum carves itself
into the roots at Osain's feet,
so he runs to el ritmo sicá.
A vejigante mask blooms
at Osain's heel.

Bronzed and patinaed,
an oxidized mangrove tree,
Osain still runs,
guardian of herbs, wizard
of plants, forest stilt-walker.
Samuel Lind plants a garden
inside his studio;

he finds a woman,
and makes a son.

> *El camino de un artista.*
> *That moment of satisfaction*
> *of touching someone.*
> *Only the love that is*
> *projected I receive.*
> *I receive love. Money*
> *does not pay. Only*
> *the love. It is to see*
> *something beyond the senses.*

He sculpts Osain
born of the marriage
of earth and water,
Osain, with one ear
that hears nothing,
and one ear that hears
leaves falling and the hum
of babies sleeping.
Osain, who brings us medicine
and healing, un botánico africano.

Samuel Lind paints nature
within prisms, tubes of light;
futuristic, vegetable visions
of Earth goddess and Osain,
of the energy and movement
ever forward of his people
of Loíza, Loíza Aldea.

SPATHES

I gather now dry-leaf spathes
that boys spear-wave
and sword-cross, float
into flooded gutters
like dugout canoes.
I arrange them on the wall
in peacock array. Hollowed
scoops that were sheathes,
wombs for palm tree florescence,
cast-off husks, now you
are canoes that we women
paddle on the brown-green river
of consciousness. I layer
spathes into a ladder
that holds my spirit weight.
One green spade I take from
my deck of playing cards. I place
it in the centre of this altar.
A shield. A crude halo
for the goddess who granted me
time on Earth and a daughter.
The father told me when I was pregnant
that the child was all that mattered.
The baby was the corn ear;
I was the husk that he would
chuck away. I gave birth, Saraswati.
I believed that I was not a husk.
Green seed, green heart.
Let my daughter receive your gifts
of music, poetry and a strong mind,
so that she, too, knows that no woman
is a husk to be tossed away,
a sword to be crossed,
a canoe to drift and drown
in any swollen gutter.

MARY HARLOTRY

I. LA VIRGEN DEL MANGLE

Eddie Ferraioli's glass nippers chip
brittle shingles of emerald-ice waterglass —
lime-green, blue-green, mossy teal-green,
wispy iridescent shards of the virgin's leaf bonnet —
each chip filled with lantern light
that frames her milky opal face, glazed red lips,
turquoise-shadowed eyelids, obsidian eyes
of la gitana, outlined with black Egyptian kohl
like one of Ziegfeld's dancing girls.

Hawk-wing stained glass, swirled
with white cloud and thunderhead grey, form
the twisted trellis of red mangrove roots
that twine her shoulders, breasts, waist, hips
and thighs, binding her into a swampy corset
that cinches the checkered tiles of her firestorm red dress.

Around her float glass seedlings,
long, narrow spikes, capped by leaf parachutes,
torpedoes of red mangrove pods. In her hands,
she balances an indigo crystal ball
that contains a bright blue dragonfly,
ready to flit through the mangrove and away
over salt flats, if the cruciform insect were not
just thorns of glass mired in mortar.

'Mary, mother of Earth's living things',
as Ferraioli has made her, stands tall
on her arching mangrove limbs, red arteries
drilling down into a world of streaky blue-copper
tiffany and terra cotta grout, hardened red earth.

She hangs in a forest-dark Chapel of Ease, lit by blue candles,
over a reflecting pool. In the nave
a quiet nun wears only garters of leaves,
her prayers cool to your touch.
Grace arrives as bliss and ache
on a red-cushioned pew built for two.

II. LA VIRGEN DE LAS ROSAS

Where does it belong, Ferraioli's mosaic
of la Virgen de las Rosas? In a Saturday café
serving squash blossoms in spring-mix salads,
where a waitress in scarlet head-tie leans
in behind you, resting the weight of a breast
on the back of your neck, to whisper
the menu into your ear? No. Not this time.

Each Mary, a hand-rasped crystal puzzle,
an Art Déco cathedral of glass and flowers,
for whom Ferraioli has shattered, with strip-cutters
and scoring knives, fragile translucent plates of glass,
true in hue to the island flora of the Antilles,
into thousands of shards, splinters enough to erect
a stained-glass Celestial City, a botanical hot-house,
where his erotic virgins and lewd angels reside.
All except one lone African – La Virgen de la Maga –
are arsenic-eating-white; all robed in a profusion
of Caribbean bush, bramble and bloom,
smutty-slivers of flowers teasing us
with flamboyant sexual botany.
                    In the names of Our Lady,
he fuses together glittering visions
of Caribbean virginity: La Virgen de la Orquídea,
La Virgen del Majó, del Anturio,
de la Canaria, del Tulipán Africano, del Flamboyán,

del Yagrumo, del Ave de Paraíso, de la Trinitaria,
de la Uva Playera, del Lirio Calla y Tigre.

Here, then, is the 'Virgin of the Roses, the mother
of mutilated women'. *Párate! Stop it!*
Before you think *I cannot skim*
another virgin's weft of rough-rolled pink quartz,
lavender and wispy sky-blue iridized, opalescent,
aurora rose-water glass and black sanded grout,
pause over this as Ferraioli wields
glaster circle-cutter and fletcher over his worktable
to chip out a sacred heart and red halo, a red crown of thorns,
and candy apple-red lipstick, matching stigmatas
that will gape like bloodied vaginas on her upturned palms,
this glass virgin is a fractured mirror where myths collide
and crash against blood-born women.

Remember a woman as slim and fragile
as a champagne glass, who adapts to a wheelchair
on the streets of San Juan. *He was jealous,*
muy celoso, is her muffled answer to
the microphone plunged into her face
by the blond *reportera* of *Super Exclusive.*
Remember Francheska Duarte, 19 years old,
who sits in her bed with covers pulled over
her missing legs. She cannot tell Puerto Rico
why her ex-novio and baby-father dropped his foot
on the gas pedal and hurled his car into her,
pinning her between two cars,
with such force that her legs could not be saved.

He received a sentence of three years.
He will walk on two legs out of the prison this year.
She became a banner child for la paz y el Jesucristo
in street marches until her father was arrested
for narco-trafficking, the mailing of a cocaine brick

through the US Mail to a Federal Agent.
Francheska, dusty, broken china doll,
swept hastily into the closets of public memory,
how are you? How is your toddling daughter now?

La Virgen de las Rosas is Ferraioli's only Mary
who gazes up en agonía, heavenward.
The rose-decked aura haloed around her head
looks like a doily of mundillo lace, patiently woven
from many wooden bobbins of pale thread by an abuela.

She shines in her tunic of roses and briars,
against a royal blue, blue willow, moon blue,
Mediterranean blue, cobalt blue, Caribbean blue,
vein blue, a forever blue background.
It is impossible to tell if she has phantom legs
under her rosy gown, but she has red toenails
on her white feet, posed Christ-like
on a pedestal of rose-thorn vines.

The pinky fingers of each hand
have been chopped off. Ivory shards
fall from her open hands like so many shark's teeth,
jagged, curved blades used for declitorización,
as Ferraioli's footnotes to his art informs us.

Ferraioli's Virgin is not a dominicana
en Puerto Rico. She is not brown –
not welded from glass called Bohio Brown,
Browntone, Caramel, Cinnamon, Cocoa Brown,
Coffee Bean, Copper Penny, Dunescape,
Electric Latte, Havana, Ginger Beer, Maple,
Root Beer, Tobacco Road, Walnut or Whiskey.
Ferraioli's rose virgin is as white
as the baby's milk teeth of Francheska's daughter.

At the bottom of a koi fish pond in a club
where small glass violins play and people, dressed only
in silk scarves, lie down on top of each other
in the warm, waist-high grass is where
we must install these two gleaming glasswork sisters,
unlucky water nymphs, dead darlings,
dollies, *corpus delicti,* white ladies floating Ophelia-like
on their backs, eyes closed, poised and without
a bruise or blood-drop on their florid gowns.

La Virgen de la Amapola was a girl
who tucked a pink hibiscus into her hair
on the way to school, where, all day, it opened out
its full-circle skirt, cried out in its quiet flower song
the girl's fresh beauty, like a papery pink megaphone.
Now a funereal spray of flamboyant poppies, burning
persimmon-orange-cranberry swirls of tiffany glass,
pale pistils and blue-green crystal leaves,
weigh down her dress. Her leaf-hair floats,
spiralled out to a halo, and a corona
of bruised croton leaves, plum, mauve,
violet, grows around her forehead
like a carnival head-dress. She's framed
by the Venetian blue tiles of the pond.

La Virgen de las Amapola,
'Mary, mother of raped women and girls',
in her stiff symmetry, how little this Virgin
must look like little dark-haired Angélica,
14 years old, found boca abajo, su ropa desgarrada.
You get it, don't you? How her face was covered
with lumps and bruises, all of her body singed
with cigarette burn-holes. Tortured,
violated, killed, como su vida fue nada,

with signs of penetration, both anal and vaginal,
and a blow to the back of her head, cranial trauma,
inflicted by a glass beer bottle tossed away
near the body, smeared with blood. What kind
of virgin could Ferraioli craft with that mottled green
or brown glass streaked with Angélica's blood?

Here is Ferraioli, with running pliers and tweezers,
bending over the slab of his worktable
like a good mortician, aligning each pearlized
blue-glass strip of the winding sheet
of La Virgen de Loto who, mummy-like,
with eyes closed and arms crossed over her chest,
rests on a bier of dark green, bronze mortar-veined
lotus leaves. She was somebody's bet, worth less
than the paper of a losing lotto ticket, and so
she was killed, discarded. Now in death,
her body returns to water, and from that body of water,
midnight-blue, many-petalled lotus flowers bloom,
like thirty giant crystal dissection tacks
pinning her down, from crown, veil and neck collar
to netted body – enchained in lotuses.
                    'Mary, mother of dead women
and girls never to be women', like Taty, 18, raped
y degollada, salvajemente ultrajada in a rural zone,
or valiant Celeste, 13, raped by her young uncle,
and then his elderly friend (*contra natura*), and then
another (based on the volume of semen discovered).
Girl child battered to death with a hand-held stone.

IV. LAS VIRGENES DEL CAFÉ O GUARDIANAS DEL BOSQUE

Let us display this most marvellous
of Ferraioli's virginal glassworks
in a large, quiet coffeehouse open to the sea

and filled with chaises and cool padded-leather divans,
a forest of well-groomed plants, where thoughtful readers
and lovers are welcomed by the heady aromas of Yaucono,
Café Alto Grande, Café Madre Isla, Café Mis Abuelos,
Café Mami, Café Crema, y las cafés artesanales
cultivated in the shadows of the mountains,
all made in Puerto Rico.

Ferraioli's Art Decó pièce-de-résistance,
these most lovely of virgin twins, skin whiter
than apple blossoms, nude and nubile,
perched back-to-back, sitting at the top
of a coffee bush, looking dreamily
over their shoulders, arched back just enough
to tempt us with their precious and precocious,
coquettish faces, long necks, delicate collar bones,
slender shoulders, teenage breasts with nipples
made of red coffee berries.

A flock of tiny, rare San Pedrito birds, tropical green
with red-feathered necks, alight on the blue glass
ladder rungs that frame these sisters
and guardians of the forest. The coffee bush's
thin branches burst with clusters of red ruby fruits,
but the added weight of the glowing virgins
doesn't break down the branches,
and their foreheads are not bowed by the garlands
of coffee branches and berries wreathing their heads.

They look like a black and white photo
of the twin dancing sisters, 'Rosie' Roszika
and 'Jenny' Janszieka Schwartz, in 1922,
posing together, lifting a diaphanous
chinchilla-lined cape high over their heads,
dreamily dazzled by their own popularity,
pursing their small rosebud lips,

the same pouty rosebuds of Ferraioli's mosaic.
Or another, in which they glance at each other,
showing off to viewers their long bare backs
and pert, black pageboy cuts.
                              Rosie and Jenny,
the Dolly Sisters, who danced with
Ziegfeld's Follies on Broadway and then did exotic
'Persian' routines all over Europe. Oh,
the excitement of double gyrations, kicks
and hip bumps got them clothed in jewellery,
once a be-ribboned Rolls Royce
left for them after a show – a life fox-trotting
with younger sons of kings, Prince George,
King Alonso of Spain and Edward, Prince of Wales.

It didn't end well for the Dollies,
Jenny hanging herself by a dressing gown sash,
and Rosie following her sister in a failed suicide
decades later. In the Twenties, was it
in the Follies Bergère, the Alcázar,
or the Moulin Rouge, where Romanian sculptor
Demetre Chiparus decided he must sculpt
the cabaret darlings? Influenced by the excavation
of Pharaoh Tutankhamun's tomb and
Sergei Diaghilev's Ballet Russe dancers, Chiparus'
belles were carved in bronze, wood, rock crystal,
lapis lazuli and ivory of the highest grade,
imported from the Belgium Congo,
cast in a long, slim, stylized Egyptian line.
Chiparus sculpted the dancing Dolly Sisters
in a perfect splendour of mirrored symmetry,
slender ivory arms lifted in arabesques over faces
so white and lit with an aura of French Art Decó,
an elephant whittled down to desk-top dancers.

Ferraioli's twin guardians of the forest
aren't just pale imitations of the French Empire

by a vitralist of an archipelago known by empires
for its coffee, exotic fruits and flowers.
Still, while his flora caribbeanizes Art Decó,
the chalk-faced women little resemble
our island women. The artist claims
to protest victimhood and defend us with these images
of Virgins, in a Spanish Roman Catholic island
where the Virgin/ Whore dichotomy must have
something to do with our fantastic rates
of domestic abuse, molestation, rape, and violent
homicide against women by their mates.

Ferraioli's women represent a Puerto Rican artist's
very heart-of-darkness-and-purity, his alibi
for weldbonding hundreds of thousands
of bright chinks of glass into Virgins,
like these guardians, his immaculate crusade.
For him, this is no Andalusian, Byzantine, Persian
semi-sacred playboy mosaic, but a vigilant hymn
to women's dignity.

What happens when you are a small boy
carried from la isla del encanto, of sun and sand,
and the blessings of la Señora de la Providencia,
from your birthplace of Santurce, to the villages
and Black Forest of Germany? Not yet a kindertot,
Eddie met family members, survivors of the Holocaust.
One enchanted summer, in 1954, he was in the playful care
of neighbourhood nymphs Anke and Elke,
identical twins, 13-years-old, and so true to Aryan
ideals, with transparent skin, cherry ripe and sunlit hair
that dragonflies bumbled around as they played together,
running into the Black Forest, bathing nude
in the forest lake – Anke and Elke and the little boy.
This was Ferraioli's Genesis.

This is how he explains why he makes
the mosaics of Virgins and flora: At mid-summer,
on the night of the summer solstice,
a great bonfire was built, where his mother went
to celebrate *Sommersonnenwende*, the end
of fertile spring. Of course, the bonfire was nothing
like the incinerators of German camps during the war.
Anke and Elke braided a floral wreath
of apple blossoms and put it on his head.
All was happily pagan, and so, aged only four
and susceptible to the warm blaze
and the late night mystic mood, Ferraioli fell asleep
near the fire and dreamed that his mother
had allowed him to walk off into the night forest,
alone on a trail lit by the moon and a silver cloud
of dragonflies that led him to a tree, where,
at its pinnacle, sat the twins, Anke and Elke,
quite nude, their bodies like electric beacons.
They were the guardians of the forest, vigilant
goddesses of a safe haven. They pointed him
to another tree, where he found branches laden
with eighteen small cages, each one containing
an apple. As he took each apple, it transformed
into a naked woman who clothed herself
with frondage and nosegays of flowers, disappearing
back into the bushes of the forest. One apple
remained, which he carried with him, gnawing on it
like a rat, as he returned to the bonfire, until
the fragrance of apple surrounded him as he slept.

This dream stayed with him after his return
to Puerto Rico, and into manhood, through art school
in New York, and his establishment of his art studio.
Although he has made many public artworks,
large mosaics in Santurce, the renovated windows
of the Sacred Heart Church, he continues

to piece together his apple-flesh Virgins,
working out in glass shards a boy's dreams
of Edenic desire, Anima Mundi, elegant
jewelled fruits, Virgins, some with vamp eyes.

V. A VISIT TO EDDIE FERRAIOLI'S ART STUDIO

The boarded-up, gutted Hotel Normandie,
once our grand pleasure hotel and ballroom,
docks like a phantom cruise ship near Balneario El Escambrón.
Beyond there Condado – a tropical Beverly Hills
of multi-millionaire's condos and tourists
– flows into El Boquerón, then the peninsula
of Old San Juan, and the 17 acres of Caribe Hilton,
built over the ruins of Fort San Gerónimo,
the Oasis Bar – where the Piña Colada was invented –
Morton's Steak House, and Olas Spa, where patrons
have Swedish massages, smothered in Coconut Bliss.
Just across the avenue, Ferriaoli's studio existed for years.
No other galleries until one reaches Old San Juan,
and not much else to walk to, he had a niche.

Floor-to-ceiling windows filled with his glass charmers,
mosaics, flower vases and crystal mosaic boxes
placed on lignum-vitae Victorian vanities invited the flâneur.
Las Virgenes del Café o Guardianas del Bosque,
the wall-sized mosaic, guarded the door –
a work he wouldn't sell – and La Virgen del Ave del Paraíso,
his tribute to Frida Kahlo, hung opposite the entrance,
alongside recent virgin mosaics of all sizes,
one suited to every budget, virgins crafted
over more than a decade, the new set
even-more-pale-skinned, with shining, white
glitter-glazed faces and high French coiffure,
head-dresses of tropical flowers. They wore
no dresses, but a few leaves, like fan-dancers.

When I visited, he was giving a class
to a group of women who sat around worktables,
each with a small block of pressboard, designing
a sea horse or a stem of Bird-of-Paradise,
a colour scheme, a squared-off template
she would use to work her first mosaic.
I asked about recent exhibitions and his poemario
Virgenes eróticas y ángeles lascivos,
and then my tongue was mortared to my mouth.
It was not the moment, in front of his acolytes,
to ask why his portraits of flora are Antillean,
but his palette of women most often porcelain white.

I wanted to ask about his role as artist
in a commissioned work, *Requiem Domesticus,*
but I could not. Three men, an artist,
a poet/ librettist and a musical composer,
were commissioned five years earlier to create
an artistic extravaganza, on the occasion
of the renovation of the grand theatre
of our public university in San Juan, and the donation
and installation of a full pipe organ. They agreed
to compose a (post)-modern requiem mass,
to draw attention to our propensity
for domestic abuse and 'femicidio',
numerous murders of women by their partners.

At the Museo de Arte Contemporáneo in Santurce,
Ferriaoli displayed twenty glass mosaic virgins,
one for each of the twenty women killed by partners
in Puerto Rico that year. Elidio La Torre Lagares
penned the libretto for the mass, a lamentation
invoking Madre Luna, Madre Una,
la Madre Eterna and la Madre de la Leche,
to eulogise women who have been mutilated,
humiliated, imprisoned, violated and destroyed.
These male artists fell back on images

of virginal motherhood and feminised natural world
to affirm woman's sacred value, on a Roman Catholic island
where statues of María abound.

It was hardly remembered by anyone
when a teenage boy tied his grandmother's feet,
wrists, and gagged her, cut off her night gown,
and raped her for a day, powering up
a buzzing circular saw every now and then,
threatening to slice-off her feet. Her terror dances
in my mind. When the meth-headed boy left
her apartment, she managed, still hog-tied, naked
and bloodied, to get to a neighbour's door.
Requiem Domesticus had no lyrical voice
to embrace a grandmother's intimate shame,
pain, and fear of obliteration.
                              In free verse and sonnets,
the mass sought catharsis, speaking of a goddess,
to memorialise – without memory –
those twenty women, twenty names on one more
check-list of names. Carlos Alberto Vázquez
composed music on a grand international scale
with imported musicians, a Cypriot soprano,
an Israeli mezzosoprano, a Russian bass,
an organist from Michigan, a Polish conductor
of the symphony of Chile, la Orquestra Sinfónica
de Puerto Rico, choirs and a children's chorus –
over two hundred musicians and singers.
I was in the audience. Very well then, why not
call on the Mother of Sad Milk, or any other
Mater Dolorosa to bring the spirit to our sorrow songs?
I, too, have created urban madonnas to bless
our troubled islands, mostly named for saints and virgins.

When I left Ferraioli's studio,
my questions tucked away under my tongue,

a man was descending a coconut tree
by the garage for hotel guests.
Around his waist, he had a thick,
aged leather strap that hugged the tree.
His pants, khaki, were bottom-frayed and stained.
His machete was tucked under one arm.
On the ground were at least fifty green jelly coconuts,
some still attached to chopped palm fronds.

While I paid my parking ticket, the man loaded cocos
into a plastic milk crate on the handlebars of his bicycle
and then filled a black plastic garbage bag, and roped down
his bulging tower. His bicycle was a wobbly caravel
with black plastic top-sails that he had to captain
by leaning around his tall cargo. A barefoot girl,
who soon climbed up behind him, was playing
in a yellow and red dress on the grass between
two tamarind trees – brown island daughter
with braided hair – a young version of my own girl.

Ferraioli did not see the tamarindo girl
with tamarind skin playing tag between one trunk
and the other. He will not fashion her from
Medalla bottles, smooth sea-glass, caracoles, crab
shells, whelks, coco husks, red coral, and Irish moss.

"Night Watch" (pp. 9-11)

In 2010, several sightings of a large, flying gargoyle were reported in Puerto Rico.

Sugar central: A "central" was a mill that processed the cane of various *haciendas*. It was centrally located in relation to the plantations.

Fiambrera: multi-level metal pots to warm and carry food. The pots connect one-on-top of the other, and have a carrying handle.

Perreando: Reggaetón dancehall. "Perro" means dog. A "doggie-style" dance.

Gatilleros of las Gárgolas, los pistoleros of a mountain cartel: gun men of the Gargoyles (the name of a Puerto Rican drug gang that operates in some of the mountainside pueblos).

Puntos de drogas: A buying and selling point for drugs.

"The Green Lantern y los Muertos Senta'os" (pp. 12-15)

Covered in both the local and international press for their unconventional manner of embalming the deceased and posing them as if alive for the viewing of the body, Funeraria Marín in Río Piedras, of the San Juan Metropolitan area, has, since 2008, prepared several bodies in this manner. The difuntos are popularly called "los muertos para'os" or "los muertos senta'os."

Los muertos senta'os: As "los muertos sentados" is pronounced and written: the seated dead.

Ernesto "Ché" Guevara: (1928-1967). Argentine revolutionary Marxist, guerrilla leader, writer, and physician. Ché travelled Latin America, gaining knowledge about the impact of colonialism, imperialism, monopoly capitalism, class struggle, and poverty; he participated in the Cuban revolution with Fidel and Raúl Castro, also serving the revolutionary government in various capacities. Involved in social struggles in other countries, he was executed by CIA-assisted forces in Bolivia.

Cabrón: bastard.

Caserío: residential neighbourhood with government-built, low-income housing.

Transformista: Usually, this refers to someone who participates in drag culture or helps other drag queens with their transformation.

Velorios: traditional wake in Puerto Rico, often including a home viewing of the body.

Este Chulo: this cool dude.

Promesa: The Puerto Rico Oversight, Management, and Economic Stability Act (2015-2016) has changed our orientation in relation to the word "Promesa": "promise."

Boricuas: another name for Puerto Ricans, based on the island's Taíno name, Borikén.

Viejitos verdes: "dirty old men"; or men who are sexual dynamos at an advanced age.

"La Cuna Blanca"; Ay, Angelito escapado; Raphy Leavitt: Raphy Leavitt (1948-2015) was the leader of the salsa group "La Selecta." He composed this song, "La Cuna Blanca" (white cradle) after a 1971 traffic accident in which he was injured and a trumpet player of the band, Luis Maysonet, was killed. After Leavitt recovered from being in a coma, he had repeated visions of a white cradle for a baby and the sounds of a baby crying. In the vision, Maysonet, dressed in black, assured Leavitt that he would continue to assist him from the other side. This song was performed at the funeral services of Renato García (Renato Green, as his community called him).

Bueno, bueno, bueno, nada de malo: Good, good, good, nothing bad.

Linterna Verde: Green Lantern.

Servicial: this is what was said of Renato García by his sister to the press when he died. Helpful, not servile, referring to Renato's willingness to help others in his community.

"Tissue Gallery" (pp. 16-18)

Douen: Eastern Caribbean folkloric character, the spirit of an unbaptized child, who has backwards feet and lives in the forest or near rivers. Douens lure children away to be their playmates.

Restos muertos: dead remains.

"La Monstrua Desnuda" (pp. 19-22)

The poem refers to two Spanish Baroque portraits painted by Juan Carreño de Miranda, *La monstrua desnuda* and *La monstrua vestida*

(1680). The subject of the paintings was six-year-old Eugenia Martínez Vallejo. *La monstrua desnuda* was displayed at the Museo de Arte in Ponce, Puerto Rico, as part of the travelling exhibition "De Greco a Goya," March 25-July 9, 2012.

Una niña gigante: a giant girl.

Quemaderos: the site for the burning of those condemned to the *auto-de-fé* during the reign of El Rey Carlos II.

Calle 13's bailarina Karlita: One of band Calle 13's videos and album covers has featured a successful dancer with achondroplasia.

La estética de lo feo: the aesthetic of the ugly.

"Come, Shadow" (pp. 23-26)

Yellow bird up high in banana tree: The phrase is remembered from my mother's voice singing along with a version of the song "Yellow Bird," as recorded by the singer John Gary, on his 1963 album *Catch a Rising Star.* However, the origin of the song is "Choucoune" (1883), by Haitian poet Oswald Durand (1840-1906), a poem in Kreyòl, in which the lonesome speaker praises a woman's beauty and laments to a bird that the woman was not true to him and is not with him now. "Ti zwazo" or "Ti zwezo" ("little bird") is referenced in the refrain. The melody of the song, a slow meringue, was composed in 1893 by New Orleans-born pianist Michel Mauléart Monton. The poem, reportedly, is based on an actual woman with whom Durand was involved. According to Louis J. Auguste, at the end of her life "she became insane and had to beg for survival."

"Winged Horse" (pp. 27-29)

Es mi derecho: "It's my right."

Rocinante: Don Quixote's horse.

Rocín: According to the Real Academia Española, "rocín" can refer to an old nag or a work horse; however, another definition is "hombre tosco, ignorante y maleducado" ("Rude, ignorant, uncouth man" – in my translation). I use the word with the second definition in mind, as well as the wordplay between meanings.

"One that Got Away" (pp. 30-32)

Ilán-ilán: (*Cananga odorata*) Ylang-Ylang. Extraordinarily sweet-smelling flowering tree.

Suárez: A manmade inland canal located in Carolina, created for the purpose of military defence.

Pescador-artesano: fisherman-artisan.

Pilones: cup-shaped wooden mortar used for making mófongo or crushing herbs.

Mofóngo: cooked, mashed plantains, sometimes garlic-flavored and stuffed with meats or shellfish.

La mano ponderosa: hand of power (of Christ), a traditional wooden carving in Puerto Rico. The image is of an open, upright hand with saints or the Christian holy family carved on the finger tips.

Stella Maris: the Virgin Mary in her manifestation as the Star of the Sea.

Fiestas patronales: festivals held in honour of specific Roman Catholic patron saints.

Nuestra Señora, Estrella de los mares/ Salvage me... guárdame: Our Mother, Star of the Seas, save or spare me... watch over me.

Medalla: a Puerto Rican beer.

"Justine Has a Few Words to Say to the Marquis de Sade" (pp. 33-36)

Gasolinera: gas station.

La Mujer de los Trovadores: the lady love-interest of the troubadours' songs.

Panadería: bakery and deli.

Dale poder a un pendejo y será tu verdugo: This is a "dicho," or proverb. Give power to a fool, and he will be your executioner.

"Night of Charcoal Sky and Sea" (pp. 37-39)

Malecón: boardwalk along the sea wall.

"Blue Stone" (pp. 40-42)

Villa Palmeras: an artistically, culturally and historically significant neighbourhood of Santurce in San Juan.

Marquesina: driveway or garage of the house used often for parties or family gatherings.

Park of the Salsa Kings (El Parque de los Salseros), which is located in Villa Palmeras, features bronze busts of the leading salsa musicians, some of whom were born in that neighbourhood. Karla Michelle's public funeral service took place there.

"He Talks to a Butterfly" (pp. 45-46)

Copulario: area of the butterfly farm designated for copulation and the care of gathered eggs and caterpillars.

Mariposa, Mariposario: butterfly and butterfly farm.

Me fascinan: They fascinate me.

Voy con el alma hecha pedazos: I am going with my soul torn to pieces. This is a line from the song, "Le Pese a Quien le Pese" by Vicente Fernández.

"Flowers and Songs" (pp. 47-49)

Campesinas, mexicanas y mujeres indígenas: Mexican peasant women and indigenous women of the countryside.

Guayaba, el epazote, el manrubio… hierba buena: guava, medical herb, horehound, herbs related to mint family.

Hacendado: the vast plantations/ranches, held by the land owners. They monopolised water resources

Corridos: a narrative form of song ballads that are usually about daily life events, history, resistance, and oppression.

La soldaderas Zapatistas: Women soldiers who fought with Emiliano Zapata Salazar (1879-1919) during the Mexican revolution. He led the Ejército Libertador del Sur in Morelos (Zapatistas) and inspired an agrarian and land redistribution movement.

"Song of the Harpy" (pp. 50-51)

DRNA: Department of Natural Resources.

Pues, mono guisa'o: So, monkey stew.

"Cardboard Oscars" (pp. 52-53)

The poem refers to Puerto Rican independence leader Oscar López Rivera, who was politically imprisoned for 35 years in the US. In 1976, he joined the Fuerzas Armadas de Liberación Nacional

(FALN), which engaged in activities to end US colonisation of the island. Bombings of public buildings and a night club in New York have been attributed to FALN. Puerto Ricans in the US and on the island conducted a massive campaign for his release from prison. Life-size cardboard cut-outs of Oscar were carried in street protests, displayed widely in public places, and used for the taking of selfies that were posted on social media by protestors. In 2017, after a period of house arrest in PR, López was freed.

Arresto domiciliario: house arrest.

Tecatos en la calle: Drug addicts in the street.

Aula Verde, a San Juan mariposario: In his prison letters López expressed his desire to witness the Monarch butterfly migrations.

Batatas: literally, "sweet potatoes," used to refer to politicians and other over-paid public employees who sponge on the government and do nothing of value for the island; the practice of being hired for whom you know and what political party you belong to.

Ecapuchados: Protestors/ resistance fighters who cover their faces with scarves, hoods or t-shirts to avoid being identified and legally or politically persecuted.

"Muse" (pp. 54-55)

Iglesía el Cielo de Fuego: The Church of Heavenly Fire.

Cuartel de Policia: police station.

Firma tu nombre en mis paredes: sign your name on my walls.

"Man Haffi Try" (pp. 58-60)

World-class lover, zagga zow: phrases borrowed from lyrics of dancehall deejay Beenie Man.

Pum pum: impolite Jamaican word for female genitals.

"At the Kiosk of La Gitana" (pp. 61-62)

Muñeco: Doll (male doll)

Papisongo: Big daddy.

Chocha: impolite Puerto Rican term for female genitals.

El perreo: "Doggie-style" reggaetón dance.

No importa si ella es una viejita: It doesn't matter if she is a little old gal.

Viejitas verdes: green elderly women; sexually vital.

Caballo: horse.

Tranquila: be calm.

Don Guapo: Mr. Handsome.

"The Flying Wallendas in Puerto Rico" (pp. 63-66)

In 1978, Karl Wallenda, patriarch of a circus family and founder of the troupe The Flying Wallendas, as well as other performing groups, fell to his death in the Condado area of San Juan, Puerto Rico, while attempting a hire-wire act between towers of the Conrad San Juan Condado Plaza Hotel (now called The Condado Plaza Hilton). This event remains in the popular memory of the island, and the hotel has placed a memorial plaque on the front of one of the towers facing Ashford Avenue. In 2011, Nik Wallenda and his mother Delilah successfully re-enacted Karl Wallenda's walk. Various other members of the Wallenda family have come to Puerto Rico to perform high-wire acts, walking over prison yards and mall parking lots. However, Nik and Delilah are the only descendants to repeat the walk that killed Karl Wallenda. Nik Wallenda has set world records as a contemporary funambulist.

"Revel Rebel" (pp. 70-72)

Coming through, coming right through: this line is borrowed from Linton Kwesi Johnson's poem about the Notting Hill Carnival "Forces of Victory."

"Pulse" (pp. 73-75)

Poem refers to 2016 Orlando nightclub hate crime shooting incident, in which Omar Marteen killed 49 people and wounded 58 others inside the establishment Pulse, on a Latin music night. Twenty-three of the slain self-identified as Puerto Rican. The epigraph is from Andre Bagoo's poem "Father's Day," from his 2017 collection *Pitch Lake* (Leeds: Peepal Tree Press).

Patophobia: "Pato" (duck) is a pejorative term for a homosexual person in Puerto Rico; homophobia.

"Centering the Galaxy from Corozal" (pp. 79-80)
Guaraguao: Red-tailed Hawk.
Vía Láctea: the Milky Way.
Su telescopio siempre estaba allí: His telescope was always there.

"Naranjito" (pp. 81-82)
Abu: nickname for "abuela", a grandmother.
Mazorcas, pastelitos, budín de pan: mazorcas, pastries, bread pudding.
Cafetales: coffee plantations.
Vámanos pa'l monte, vámanos pa' allá: lyrics from the song by Eddie
    Palmieri, "Vámanos pa'l monte." Let's go to the mountains; let's
    go there.

"Chairman of the Committee on Nomenclature" (pp. 83-84)
La gente: the people.

"Memoir of Repairs to the Colony" (pp. 85-87)
Leprocomio Insular: leprosy colonies and residential facilities in Puerto
    Rico were called "leprocomios."

"Vieques, 1961: The filming of *The Lord of the Flies*" (pp. 88-
    92)
The section of the poem that refers to the off-screen taunts of the boy
    actors against the actor who played Piggy is based on an online
    interview with the director of the film, Peter Brook.
La Isla Nena: What Vieques is called, as a smaller sister island of
    Puerto Rico.

"En el Cementerio Búsqueda" (pp. 93-94)
Naufragio: shipwreck.

"Campeonato de Trujillo Alto" (pp.95-98)
Poco translación: little side-to-side motion. A Paso Fino is judged to be
    more classic fino if there is little side-to-side motion in its
    movement.
Jínete: rider.

Los cascos tocan: the hooves knock (make sound).

Afro-boricua pueblo: Puerto Rican pueblo of Loíza has a majority population of African descended citizens.

"Art Brut", III. (pp. 105-109)

Novia: girl friend.

Cabrones: bastards.

"Osain" (pp. 110-112)

The poem refers to a bronze sculpture of Osain, by the Puerto Rican artist of Loíza, Samuel Lind (also the cover artist for this collection). The sculpture is installed in *La Arboleda Ancestral Africana* of the botanical gardens of Caguas, Puerto Rico.

El espíritu del bosque: the spirit of the forest.

El ritmo sicá: one of the basic rhythms of the drumming, dancing and singing tradition of bomba.

Un botánico africano: African herbal knowledge and remedies.

"Spathes" (pp. 113)

This poem responds to an art installation project by Trinidadian artist Wendy Nanan that made use of paper mâché, shells and palm tree pods, a poetic sequence and photos by Andre Bagoo, and a curatorial project by Marsha Pearce. My sequence from which this poem came was on exhibition April 7-May 5, 2016, with Nanan's art, at Medulla Art Gallery in Port of Spain, Trinidad & Tobago.

"Mary Harlotry" (pp. 114-127)

The poems in this sequence refer to glass mosaic works by the vitralist Eddie Ferraioli in his series of twenty Virgins adorned with Puerto Rican flora. Photographs of the specific works referred to may be seen in *Poui: The Cave Hill Literary Annual*, Volume 16, December 2015 (pp. 10-22), where the poem sequence was first published (available online).

"La Virgen del Mangle" (pp.114): The Virgin of the Mangrove.

"La Virgen de las Rosas" (pp. 115-117): The Virgin of the Roses.

La Virgen de la Maga: Maga (*Thespesia grandiflora*) is also called Maga in English.

La Virgen de la Orquídea; La Virgen del Majó; del Anturio; de la Canaria; del Tulipán Africano; del Flamboyán; del Yagrumo; del Ave de Paraíso; de la Trinitaria; de la Uva Playera; del Lirio Calla y Tigre: *La Orchída* is the orchid; *El Majó* is the blue mahoe; *El Anturio* is the anthurium; *La Canaria* is the allamanda or yellow trumpet; *El Tulipán Africano* is the African Tulip; *El Flamboyán* is the Royal Poinciana or flamboyant tree; *El Yagrumo* is the same in English; *El Ave de Paraíso* is the Bird of Paradise; *La Trinitaria* is the bougainvillea; *La Uva Playera* is the sea grape; *El Lirio Calla y Tigre* are the Calla and Tiger lilies.

Párate: Stop!

He was jealous, muy celoso: He was jealous, very jealous.

Reportera: reporter.

Agonía: agony.

Mundillo: a type of fine hand-crafted white lace made from knot tying on a cylindrical tube with many threaded wooden bobbins (shuttles) and stick pins.

La abuela: grandmother.

Declitorización: removal of the clitoris.

"La Virgen de la Amapola y la Virgen del Loto" (pp. 118-119): The Virgin of the Hibiscus and the Virgen of the Lotus.

Boca abajo, su ropa desgarrada: face down and her clothes torn.

Como su vida fue nada: as if her life were nothing.

Degollada, salvajemente ultrajada en una zona rural: throat slit, savagely ravaged in a country area.

Contra natura: in a manner against nature.

"Las Vírgenes del Café o Guardianas de Bosque" (pp. 119-123): The Virgins of Coffee or Guardians of the Forest.

Los cafés artesanales: artisan-produced coffees.

"A Visit to Eddie Ferraioli's Art Studio" (pp. 124-127)

Virgenes eróticas y ángeles lascivos: *Erotic Virgins and Lascivious Angels*, the title of a poetry collection written by Eddie Ferraioli.

Madre Luna, Madre Una, la Madre Eterna and la Madre de la Leche: Mother of the Moon, the one Mother, Eternal Mother and Mother of Milk.

Mater Dolorosa: the enduring and suffering Mother.

Caracoles: snails.

ABOUT THE AUTHOR

Loretta Collins Klobah lives in San Juan, Puerto Rico, where she is a professor of Caribbean literature, creative writing and medical humanities at the University of Puerto Rico. She earned an M.F.A. in poetry writing from the Writers' Workshop at the University of Iowa, where she also completed a doctoral degree in English, with an emphasis in Caribbean literature. Her poetry collection *The Twelve-Foot Neon Woman* (Leeds: Peepal Tree Press, 2011) received the 2012 OCM Bocas Prize in Caribbean Literature in the category of poetry and was short-listed for the 2012 Felix Dennis Prize for Best First Collection in the Forward Prize series. She has been awarded the Pushcart Prize for Poetry, the Earl Lyons Award from The Academy of American Poets, the Pam Wallace Award for an Aspiring Woman Writer, the *Daily News* Prize for Poetry from *The Caribbean Writer*, and the Tom McAfee Discovery Award from *The Missouri Review*. She was also a recipient of a tuition scholarship at Breadloaf Writers' Conference at Middlebury College in Vermont. Her poems have appeared in *The New Yorker, BIM, Caribbean Beat Magazine, The Caribbean Writer, The Caribbean Review of Books, Poui: The Cave Hill Literary Annual, Susumba's Book Bag, Moko: Caribbean Arts and Letters, WomanSpeak, TriQuarterly Review, Quarterly West, Black Warrior Review, The Missouri Review, The Antioch Review, Cimarron Review, A Congeries of Poetry at Connotation Press, Live Encounters, Simple Past, Smartish Pace, Vox Populi, Ekphrastic Review, PNR* and *Poet Lore.* Her poetry has been anthologized in *Best American Poetry 2016*, edited by David Lehman and Edward Hirsch; *New Caribbean Poetry: An Anthology,* edited by Kei Miller; *Under the Volcano/ Bajo el volcán*, edited by Magda Bogin; *Puerto Rico en mi Corazón,* edited by Erica Mena, Raquel Salas-Rivera, and Ricardo Maldonado; *TriQuarterly New Writers,* edited by Reginald Gibbons and Susan Hahn; and *How Much Earth,* edited by Christopher Buckley.

ALSO BY LORETTA COLLINS KLOBAH

The Twelve-Foot Neon Woman
ISBN: 9781845231842; pp. 102; pub. 2011; price £8.99

Loretta Collins Klobah gives us a twelve-foot woman with red neon surging through her veins, who boldly and gracefully takes on the challenges of urban life. Against a soundtrack of world music, from salsa to reggae to jazz, and in a vibrant blend of English, Spanish and patois, she delivers both tender and incendiary hymns of homage to the Caribbean, America and London.

Scrutinizer, witness, and warner woman, she turns her electric gaze on the everyday world and its extraordinary people. In poems that are lyrical, narrative, sensual and often experimental, she whispers curses against bad-mindedness, sings chants of prophecy, recites praisesongs to the radiance of rebellion and wails lamentations for those men, women and children who have been annihilated, lost or forgotten. There are quiet mediations, too, upon the lives of girl children, women in precarious situations, older women and enduring friendships between women.

The world of her poems is urban and aggressively contemporary, but she sees the enduring presence of splendid, though endangered, nature and of the spirit-world, which together offer green-hearted hope for the future and the possibility of cultural metamorphosis.

"Collins Klobah hears language… beautifully. In her ear English and Spanish, Bob Marley and Miles Davis, Derek Walcott and the midnight utterances of a graffitied woman all meet and make sense together. With such masterful coordination of sound, it is little wonder that these poems work on the page but also rise up from it (much like the twelve-foot neon woman in the centre of the collection), and pronounce their way into the world." — Kei Miller

"*The Twelve-Foot Neon Woman* is a remarkable contribution to Caribbean literature." — Mervyn Morris